HIX

Oyster & Chop House

MARK HIX

PHOTOGRAPHS BY JASON LOWE

QUADRILLE

INTRODUCTION

After working for 18 years or so in some of the UK's most talked about restaurants, with legendary restaurateurs King and Corbin – to get places like Le Caprice, The Ivy and Scott's back on the London restaurant map – I decided it was time to venture off on my own. Of course, I had to leave a fantastic team behind me, as it's not considered etiquette to rape previous restaurants of all their staff, although this does happen occasionally.

Ratnesh Bagdai, previously finance director at Caprice Holdings, had been badgering me for a while to do something together. Finally, when the old Rudland & Stubbs site became available, I knew it could be the opportunity we had been waiting for. Having an accountant as a business partner is a big advantage with a restaurant. It allows me to concentrate on the creative side, while Ratnesh and his wife Niketa's team look after the rest of the business. Neglecting to keep up with all that stuff is often why a restaurant fails and closes.

Rudland & Stubbs had been an established fish restaurant on the site, which is a stone's throw from London's Smithfield meat market, since the late seventies, but when we acquired the premises early in 2008 it was in need of a new lease of life. We decided to focus the restaurant on the produce the locality is so famous for – meat – and my favourite oysters.

My mate Fergus Henderson, who is similarly centred on British meat, had opened his restaurant, St John, in the area over a decade ago – to great acclaim. Friendly local competition is always a good thing and when I mentioned

to Fergus what I was proposing to do, in the Groucho Club one evening, he chuckled and swiftly ordered a round of Negronis to celebrate his new neighbour.

I was keen to evoke the atmosphere of London's traditional oyster and chop houses, where you could sample the very best of the season's oysters and a variety of meat cuts. Meat on the bone would be the trademark of this new venture, I decided. Risky perhaps, but no one had really done it before. The interior of the restaurant with its long, well-worn marble bar, tiles and wooden partitioning was well suited to the idea.

In the 1800s, chop houses were popular, civilised places to eat big chunks of meat. And oysters were once cheap London street food. In the good old days, you could sit at a tavern bar and eat oysters to your heart's content, but the custom died out in London when they became prohibitively expensive. That was until the Wright Brothers and Richard Corrigan started the oyster revival a few years back.

So, an oyster and chop house it was to be. I was somewhat hesitant to stick my name above the door, but Ratnesh and Clare Lattin, my long-term partner, twisted my arm and now I can see that it makes perfect sense. It's certainly different – my surname is more or less obsolete in the telephone directory.

We didn't have much money between us, but with a little help from the bank we managed to scrape enough cash together to do a modest refurb. Clare was my buffer for ideas and a huge help in sourcing stuff – from the Duralex glasses to the antique coat hooks. Many of the original features remain intact, however, including the long bar and the wooden flooring and panelling. With the addition of a few quirky pieces of art, including the Noble and Webster neon from the Rivington (see page 192... you'll need a mirror to read it), and some clever vintage silverware from Margolis, our silverware supplier, the place began to take on a distinctive, informal character of its own.

Together with my Head Chef, Stuart Tattershall, we somehow managed to round up a great team and open in April 2008. Most of the original staff are still with me today. It can be difficult to persuade an ambitious chef to adopt a simple brief – designed to fulfill a specific concept – as so many are set on gaining those red stars. But Stuart understood my philosophy. For me, sourcing great ingredients and doing as little to them as possible – so customers can fully appreciate their true flavours and textures – is a skill in itself. And it's a challenge to evolve the menu with the seasons, continually making the most of great British produce.

Inevitably, there were a few teething problems to begin with, particularly with the service, but we were well reviewed on our food from day one. It was an encouraging start, not least because Hix Oyster & Fish House was due to open in the summer in Lyme Regis, West Dorset, close to my roots. Two years down the line both restaurants are running smoothly and we've recently opened another, Hix, in London's Soho.

However, it isn't just the restaurant business that interests me, I'm equally keen to promote simple, honest cooking at home. The dishes we prepare and cook at the Oyster & Chop House are straightforward and easy to replicate in a home kitchen, so I feel it's time to share them with you.

OYSTERS

Surprisingly perhaps, for a country where oysters were once sold on the streets as cheap food, we are no longer a nation of serious oyster eaters. Of course, we do still eat oysters, but to nowhere near the same extent as the French. There are many oyster fisheries around our coastlines, including a fair number on historic oyster farming sites, but you will rarely find an oyster shack or nearby restaurant serving them as you would across the Channel.

Oysters may no longer be cheap, but they deserve to be celebrated – as a simple bar snack or part of a main meal. The Wright Brothers' Oyster & Porter House in London's Borough market is a great place to eat and socialise and I'm hoping that more oyster bars will start to appear around the country for people to enjoy the fruits of the sea with friends.

In the Oyster & Chop House we like to offer customers a choice and it's not unusual to see five or six varieties chalked up on the board at any one time. Our oysters are all from the UK and Ireland – natives and cultivated rock oysters, as well as tiny pearl oysters. We sell them per oyster, which gives the customer the opportunity to order one of each. It's a great way to appreciate the subtle differences in flavour, which vary with the time of the year as well as the variety of oyster.

I am constantly amazed how oyster farming and fishing varies so much around the country. I don't think I've been to two oyster farms that use exactly the same method. All manner of traditional and modern techniques are employed by oyster farmers to get the best from their local beds.

DUCHY OF CORNWALL OYSTERS For a city lawyer and a music producer, the Wright Brothers – Ben Wright and Robin Hancock – have done pretty well supplying oysters from France, the UK and Ireland to many of London's top restaurants, and acquiring the Duchy of Cornwall oyster farm on the Helford river.

The Duchy is one of very few private oyster fisheries left in this country. Port Navas Creek, where the Duchy oysterage joins the Helford river, is HQ and the oysters are sorted, graded and purified under Ben's watchful eye, ready to be transported to London and France.

Oysters have been grown on the Helford river for a few centuries now and evidence of oyster fishing dates back to the second and third centuries when the Celts first settled and built coastal forts during the Roman invasions.

Once the source of the majority of oysters in the UK, Helford oyster stocks were sadly depleted through neglect and fuel pollution over the years, like many other oyster fisheries around the coast. However, the river is now a marine conservation area and with voluntary help from the local community and Ben's hard work the oysters have made a comeback.

A new cage cultivation technique is currently being pioneered, which involves growing several nets of oysters in cages, enabling them to be easily lifted from the river bed on any tide.

The Duchy of Cornwall oyster farm is now producing Frenchman's Creek rocks from the tributary of the Helford; Helford Natives (illustrated on page 17), which the late Keith Floyd claimed were his favourite; and Duchy Specials (also illustrated on page 17), which are plump rock oysters from the Helford.

THE OYSTERS OF COLCHESTER Believe it or not Colchester, or Camulodunum as it was known then, was the capital of Roman Britain. It may not be much of a gastronomic haven these days, but it is still the capital of oyster cultivation.

The Romans adored oysters, revering them as a delicacy, and traded those that grew in the creeks surrounding Camulodunum. Not only did they transport them around the country, they also took them across the Channel, keeping them alive in roped sacks towed behind their ships. Oyster shells found in excavations provide evidence of the Romans love of our native oysters.

After the Romans departure, early in the fifth century, the status of the oyster declined and they became merely a cheap alternative to meat. Even so, up to the mid-nineteenth century, there was still a thriving oyster industry on the Blackwater and other estuaries along the Essex coast. Oysters were transported by boats, which sailed round the coast and up the Thames, mooring at Billingsgate. Their catch would fetch low prices, before being sold as cheap street food in the East End and in ale houses.

As the rail network developed, the demand for oysters grew across the country and subsequent over-fishing diminished stocks. The problem was further exacerbated by pollution from sewage that was being flushed into the estuary.

The demand for oysters may not be what it was in Roman times, but our coastal waters are much cleaner and there has been a revival of the industry in the area. In and around Colchester I've come across some great oyster producers.

MALDON OYSTERS A decade ago on a chilly autumn morning I went onto the Blackwater to shoot some wild fowl, forage some wild sea vegetables and gather a few oysters once the tide was fully out. As I waded out with a friend into the silty estuary to search for native and rock oysters camouflaged in the grey sand, we were totally alone in the peaceful tidal estuary, gathering food for free. Had we been in France, we most certainly wouldn't have been alone.

Maldon, which is southwest of Colchester, is famous for its sea salt marshes and, of course, highly prized Maldon sea salt, but it also has oysters.

The Maldon Oyster Company, which started up in 1960, was originally owned by a cooperative of local fishermen and run by Clarrie Devall. The icy winter of 1963 killed off a lot of the oysters, but Devall started growing new stocks a few years later in Goldhanger Creek off the Blackwater.

In the early 1980s Devall teamed up with David Coward-Talbott and started growing rock oysters (illustrated on page 20) on the old oyster beds, plus small quantities of natives in the main Blackwater. After Devall sadly passed away in 2002, Coward-Talbott formed the Maldon Oyster and Seafood Company with local businessman Richard Emans.

Since Coward-Talbott's retirement, the company has been run by Richard and Caroline Emans, who are successfully farming oysters on about 3500 acres of the Blackwater.

They have built a swanky modern shellfish holding and purification plant at Cock Clark near Maldon. They also use an eco-harvester, which harvests shellfish without damage to the estuary bed. It's great to see an area that was once a huge source of oysters brought back to something of its former glory.

WEST MERSEA OYSTERS There are still a fair few serious oystermen on the island of West Mersea, to the south of Colchester. Richard Haward, for example, continues his family's tradition, which dates back to 1792, of harvesting native oysters and taking them up to London to sell.

Richard's wife Heather runs The Company Shed, one of my favourite eateries in West Mersea, which serves simply prepared great local seafood. You can also sample Richard's oysters at his oyster bar on Fridays and Saturdays in London's Borough Market. Haward specialises in natives, but 70 per cent of what he sells is the all-year-round rock oyster (illustrated on page 18).

Another successful local trader, Christopher Kerrison of The Colchester Oyster Fishery, grows oysters in the upper part of the Pyfleet Creek, just behind Mersea Island. A few years ago Christopher started marketing Colchester Piccolos (illustrated on page 18), which are half-size versions of the rock oyster, rather like a cocktail oyster I once come across in New York's Grand Central Oyster Bar called the Kumamoto.

Just down the road is Mike Dawson's West Mersea Oyster company. Mike worked for a local oyster farmer when he left school until he set up his own company in 1990. Each year he sells about 70 tons of natives (illustrated on page 19) and has beds on the Blackwater and surrounding creeks.

Mike reckons that natives can be quite temperamental and when we have really extreme weather conditions they just don't hold up. He tells me that certain wider, deeper parts of the creeks are just too cold for the oysters, whereas the shallower, narrower parts of the creek tend to be a bit warmer and more conducive for natives.

Like many other oyster farmers in the UK, Mike deals in a certain percentage of rock oysters, which are much sturdier in these extreme conditions and grow more quickly. He also grows a smaller species, which he has called the West Mersea Pearl (illustrated on page 19).

Like Richard Haward, Mike Dawson has set up an oyster bar, where you can buy his oysters, lobster, and fantastically fresh deep-fried fish and chips. With traders like this, West Mersea is becoming one of the best places on the coast to eat really simple local fish and seafood and it makes a good day out for the family.

LINDISFARNE OYSTERS I'm quite surprised that the Northeast is a bit of a desert when it comes to oyster farming. Christopher and Helen Sutherland run the only oyster farm on the northeast coast on a site that was established by the monks of the Lindisfarne Priory. There is even evidence to suggest that oyster beds existed as far back as 1381 when the monks bought an oyster-filled boat for 100 shillings from a Scotsman. In the late 1800s there was an attempt by the Tankerville family to revive the oyster beds, but financial problems led to their demise again.

The Sutherlands' oyster farm is a fairly recently revived venture, started up in 1989 by Christopher's father, John, who farmed the land. At low tide, John discovered oysters shells and decided to have a go at farming at sea, too.

The oyster farm is situated between Ross, near Bamburgh, and Holy island in Northumberland. Natives and rock oysters (illustrated on page 20) are both harvested.

I just love the way that oyster farming techniques are so diverse, with similar end results. Christopher and Helen have a pretty special amphibious oyster barge – similar to Gary's down in Poole, but without the sophisticated dredger as the oysters here are accessible at low water... well fairly accessible.

In this case the barge enables the oysters to be swiftly harvested from the trestles where they are grown in sacks in the water; it can also manoeuvre around on land to transport the oysters back along the mud flats to their home farm a couple miles away. It's a fairly new vehicle, which they had built in France at La Tremblade to replace their old land rover and trailer. It makes life easier and less labour intensive and, with fewer journeys back and forth, more environmentally friendly.

LOCH RYAN OYSTERS David and Tristan Hugh-Jones have been well-known names on the oyster scene in London for as long as I can remember. They took control of the largest natural native oyster beds in the country up on Loch Ryan in Stranraer,

Scotland, in 1996, which have been fished since they were given to The Wallace family by King William 111 in 1701. The natives (illustrated on page 21) are dredged from September to April and are often among the first to appear on London restaurant menus.

I spent a few hours on the oyster dredger with Tristan and the crew on a rainy autumn Sunday. Although these may well be the largest purely native beds in the UK, the yield of sellable oysters was remarkably small by the time they had been dredged and hand graded on board by the crew and Tristan. The other 90 per cent or so get loaded into baskets to be re-layed in different parts of the loch to grow and naturally re-spawn. Some of these oysters will take up to 3 to 5 years to reach market size and in the meantime provide good surfaces for new spat to settle on. Many oyster farms around the country will buy in oyster seed and juvenile oysters to grow, but on Loch Ryan they just do their own thing. We sunk a few fine fresh-out-of-the-water natives for lunch on the boat, washed down with, ironically, a bottle of well chosen Oyster Bay Sauvignon Blanc. It was all that was needed to go with the oysters – no Tabasco, lemon or shallot vinegar. To my mind, natives should be eaten for what they are.

PORTLAND OYSTERS When I'm at the Oyster & Fish House in Lyme Regis, I love it when customers ask where the oysters are from. I just point across Lyme Bay on a clear day towards Portland and say, 'Just over there.' Even if it's not clear, I still point at the sea mist and wait for their reaction!

After a long absence, oyster farming on the Fleet lagoon, which lies behind Chesil Beach and runs between Abbotsbury and Wyke Regis, started up again around 30 years ago and Nigel Bloxham took over the oyster farm in 2005. Nigel trained as a chef and has a total passion for the fruits of the sea. When he took over the oyster beds, Nigel inherited a wooden beach café, which he has sympathetically revamped with pink frilly umbrellas outside and straw hats dotted around for when the sun is out. Nigel's Crab House Café has become a local destination for simple seafood dining. Nigel and I look at each other's establishments as an enhancement for the area, rather then local competition. He supplies us with oysters and we eat and drink in each other's establishments, exchanging fishy stories over a drink or two.

The oyster farm that Nigel inherited was rather run down at the time. To protect the oysters from the strong current of the tidal Fleet estuary – and for ease of harvesting – the rock oysters where grown in nets on old metal trestles. Nigel has replaced all the rusted old supports with wooden ones, which avoids the obvious potential pollution.

More recently, Nigel has been experimenting with new Australian plastic-meshed baskets – neat little things that rock on the trestles as the tide agitates them, so the oysters don't attach themselves to each other. We occasionally take small half-sized oysters from Nigel, which we call Portland pearls (illustrated on page 21); these are a perfect size for handing around at cocktail parties.

BROWNSEA ISLAND OYSTERS Unlike many of the oyster beds around the country, those of Othniel Oysters, which are situated just off Brownsea Island in Poole harbour, are not actually visible. So Gary Wordsworth harvests his oysters with a mechanical dredger – an eco-harvester, designed by himself, which gently moves over the oyster beds bringing the oysters up on a conveyor belt onto the deck, where they are then graded by hand by Gary.

It's a simple two-man operation harvesting the oysters and getting them to Gary's HQ, called Number 3, which is the old Sandbanks Ferry, now anchored close to the oyster beds. Gary managed to persuade the harbour master to let him use the anchored-up car ferry for his business as it was out of sight of residential properties and a seaworthy, environmentally-friendly enterprise.

Number 3 has been kitted out with everything for oyster processing, including spare parts to get his eco-harvester back up and running in an emergency. Surrounding Gary's old ferry are baskets of graded oysters awaiting shipment off to nearby Pete Miles' Dorset Oysters depuration plant where they are purified for 42 hours. Pete is also a local fisherman and has a fish restaurant too.

Along with the natives and standard sized rock oysters (both illustrated on page 22), Gary also harvests a lot of very large rocks, which he sells to Asia; these are ideal for our oyster stew.

DUCHY SPECIALS

HELFORD NATIVES

COLCHESTER ROCKS

COLCHESTER PICCOLOS

WEST MERSEA NATIVES

WEST MERSEA PEARLS

MALDON ROCKS

LINDISFARNE ROCKS

LOCH RYAN NATIVES

PORTLAND PEARLS

BROWNSEA ISLAND ROCKS

BROWNSEA ISLAND NATIVES

HOW TO SHUCK AN OYSTER

Lay the oyster in a folded cloth on a flat surface with the flat part of the shell uppermost and hold it firmly. Force the point of an oyster knife into the hinge of the shell and carefully move the knife from side to side to prise open the shell.

Run the knife along the top of the flat shell, twisting it slightly, until you reach the muscle that attaches the oyster to the shell. Sever this and lift off the top shell.

Remove any fragments of shell from the oyster flesh, but be careful to retain the juices. The oyster will still be attached to the lower shell by the rest of the muscle. Most chefs cut through this and turn the oyster over but I prefer to leave this to the customer.

Serve on a bed of seaweed or crushed ice, with lemon wedges and/or Tabasco sauce.

OYSTER STEW

I'm not that keen on cooking oysters, but when you are confronted with large specimens that are slightly overwhelming, even for the keenest of oyster lovers, they are well suited to a dish like this. Milky oysters would be ideal here, too. This is a popular dish in the States.

Serves 4

50g butter

1 medium onion, peeled and finely chopped

100g piece of rindless streaky bacon, cut into rough 1cm pieces

1 tbsp plain flour

½ glass of dry white wine

1 litre fish stock

2 celery sticks, cut into rough 1cm pieces

salt and freshly ground white pepper

1 leek, cut into rough 1cm pieces, washed

300g waxy potatoes, peeled and cut into rough 1cm cubes

100ml double cream

2 tbsp chopped parsley

12 large oysters, shucked, juices reserved (see page 23)

Melt the butter in a large saucepan and gently cook the onion and bacon for 3–4 minutes without colouring until soft, stirring every so often. Stir in the flour and cook over a low heat for 30 seconds, then stir in the wine.

Gradually stir in the fish stock to avoid lumps forming, then bring to the boil. Add the celery and season with salt and pepper. Lower the heat and simmer for 20 minutes.

Add the leek and potatoes and simmer for a further 8–10 minutes or until the potatoes are tender. Ladle one-fifth of the soup into a blender and purée until smooth, then stir back into the soup.

Add the cream, chopped parsley and oysters together with any juices, re-season if necessary and simmer for another 2–3 minutes before serving.

OYSTER MARY

There's something of a 'morning after' trait about oysters and the idea of sliding down one topped with frozen bloody Mary is a bit of a sobering thought. You can make your bloody Mary mix as spicy as you wish, and even use it with other raw shellfish like queen scallops or clams.

Serves 4

12 rock oysters, shucked, juices reserved (see page 23)

For the bloody Mary
200ml tomato juice

30–50ml vodka, or less if you wish

1 tbsp Worcestershire sauce, or less if you wish

juice of ½ lemon

a couple of drops of Tabasco, or to taste

1 tbsp freshly grated horseradish, or to taste

celery salt

To serve
seaweed or rock salt

First mix all of the ingredients for the bloody Mary together in a bowl, adjusting the seasoning and spiciness to taste. Transfer to a freezerproof container and place in the freezer for 2–3 hours, stirring every 45 minutes or so as it freezes. Once frozen, break it up into small crystals with a spoon then return to the freezer until required.

To serve, place the oysters in their half-shell on a bed of seaweed or rock salt on serving plates. Spoon the frozen bloody Mary on top of the oysters to serve.

BAR

These days a customer is just as likely to have a great time eating at a bar seat as at a table in a restaurant. We don't have a bar menu as such, but I have a selection of dishes at the top of the menu that can be eaten with drinks on arrival, or just nibbled on while hanging out at the bar. Often it's something as simple yet sophisticated as a gull's egg with mayonnaise, fennel and celery salt, but I also like to include the odd surprise, such as fried broad bean pods. Most of our bar snacks have a seasonal element, not least fresh peas in their pods and heritage radishes, and quite a few are deep-fried, which helps to achieve that savoury nibbling element.

In its previous life as Rudland & Stubbs, the restaurant was a regular destination for lawyers and city boys, who would sit at the bar and order oysters and a drink or two. The week we opened a suited customer walked straight past me at reception to the end of the bar and sat down. I went over and introduced myself but didn't have the nerve to ask him if he had booked. Roy Walkden promptly told me that the seat he had perched on was his and had been for 20 years. 'Of course,' I said and 'lovely you are trying us.' He loved the gull's eggs on the menu – offered by the bowl so you can help yourself to as many as you want. Roy dines with us a couple of times a week and orders the same – a dozen natives, gull's eggs (when in season) and a glass of Champagne.

I view the bar culture as important. For me it breaks up the informality of a restaurant and makes it real. The bar man, of course, plays a big role, being the entertainer and waiter.

DEEP-FRIED BROAD BEAN PODS

I discovered this recent addition to the menu by fluke when I tried deep-frying broad bean pods instead of throwing them in the compost. It seems such a waste to chuck away so much of what you buy. They were suprisingly good so I did another batch, this time spicing the flour up a little with cumin and paprika... equally delicious.

Serves 6–8

8–10 empty young broad bean pods
salt and freshly ground black pepper
120–150g self-raising flour
150ml milk
vegetable or corn oil for deep-frying
Cornish sea salt for sprinkling

Cut or tear the bean pods in half lengthways along the natural seam and remove any stringy bits and discoloured ends. Cut the pods into 3–4cm lengths. Season the flour generously (spice it up a bit as well if you like, as suggested above).

Have 3 bowls ready, one with the seasoned flour, one for the milk and the third for the finished bean pods. Heat an 8cm depth of oil in a deep-fat fryer or other suitable deep, heavy pan to 160–180°C.

Coat the pods in the flour, shaking off any excess, then pass them through the milk and again through the flour. Deep-fry the bean pods in batches, stirring occasionally, for 3–4 minutes until lightly coloured and crisp. Remove with a slotted spoon and drain on kitchen paper. Immediately sprinkle with sea salt and serve.

HERITAGE RADISHES WITH MAYONNAISE

Radishes make a great bar snack or a nibble with drinks before lunch or dinner. There are several interesting varieties on the market these days, so buy a couple of different types if possible. If you are a gardener you can, of course, easily grow your own.

Serves 6–8

2–3 bunches of radishes

For the mayonnaise
2 free-range egg yolks (at room temperature)
2 tsp white wine vinegar
1 tsp English mustard
2 tsp Dijon mustard
½ tsp salt
freshly ground white pepper
100ml olive oil mixed with 200ml vegetable oil
squeeze of lemon, to taste (optional)

To prepare the radishes, remove any dead leaves and give them a good wash in cold water. Drain well and pat dry on kitchen paper.

To make the mayonnaise, put the egg yolks, wine vinegar, mustards, salt and pepper into a bowl (don't use an aluminium one, as it will turn the mayonnaise grey). Stand the bowl on a damp cloth to stop it slipping and mix well with a whisk.

Now gradually trickle the oils into the bowl, whisking continuously. If the mayonnaise is getting too thick, add a few drops of water and continue whisking in the oil. When it is all incorporated, taste and re-season if necessary and add a little lemon juice if you like.

Serve the radishes on a platter, with the mayonnaise in a bowl alongside, for dipping.

VEGETABLE CRISPS

These are worth the effort even if they do take a little time to prepare. My favourites are celeriac and parsnip crisps. Beetroot crisps look spectacular, though they are trickier to get really crisp. A combination of all three makes a great bar snack.

Serves 8

1 small head of celeriac, peeled
1 large parsnip, scrubbed clean
1 large beetroot, peeled
vegetable or corn oil for deep-frying
sea salt

Using a mandolin or swivel vegetable peeler, cut the celeriac, parsnip and beetroot into wafer-thin slices, then pat the vegetable strips dry on kitchen paper.

Heat approximately an 8cm depth of oil in a deep-fat fryer or other suitable deep, heavy pan to 180°C.

Deep-fry the vegetable slices, a handful at a time, for 2–3 minutes until lightly coloured and just starting to crisp; stir them around in the oil to ensure that they cook evenly and don't stick together.

Using a slotted spoon, transfer the vegetable crisps to a rack lined with kitchen paper and immediately sprinkle with sea salt. Leave them to dry somewhere warm but not hot – they will continue to crisp up as they dry – while you deep-fry the rest. Serve the crisps as soon as possible.

SCOTCH QUAIL'S EGGS

Good-quality sausage and haggis are essential for these neat little bar snacks. Bought sausage meat is often poor quality so I'd recommend buying Cumberland sausages and removing the skins. Mayonnaise (see page 28) – flavoured with chopped capers, mustard or herbs, or all three – is the ideal accompaniment.

Makes 12

12 quail's eggs
125g good-quality Cumberland sausage meat
125g haggis
2–3 tbsp plain flour
1 free-range egg, beaten
40–50g fresh white breadcrumbs
vegetable oil for deep-frying

Bring a pan of water to the boil and carefully lower the quail's eggs in, using a slotted spoon. Cook for 1½ minutes. Drain and cool under the cold tap for a minute or so, then carefully peel.

Mix the sausage meat and haggis together and divide into 12 balls, then flatten into patties. Wrap one around each quail's eggs, moulding it with your hands to coat evenly.

Have 3 shallow bowls ready, one with flour, one with the egg and the third with the breadcrumbs. One at a time, coat the eggs with the flour first, shaking off excess, then put through the egg and finally into the breadcrumbs, turning them to coat all over and re-moulding as necessary.

Heat a 6cm depth of oil in a deep-fat fryer or other suitable deep, heavy pan to 140–150°C. Deep-fry the eggs for 4–5 minutes, turning them every so often to colour evenly. Remove with a slotted spoon and drain on kitchen paper.

Serve the Scotch quail's eggs whole or halved, with a flavoured mayonnaise.

QUAIL'S EGG SHOOTERS

One of my favourite restaurants in New York, the Fatty Crab, offers these with Southeast Asian flavourings, but they work equally well with British flavours – like crisp bacon and chives. Vary the toppings as the mood takes you. For the restaurant I've had some wooden boards made with cavities to hold the eggs, but you can just sit them in coarse sea salt.

Serves 4

2 rashers of smoked streaky bacon, rind removed
2 tsp finely chopped chives
12 quail's eggs
coarse sea salt

Grill or fry the bacon rashers until crisp, let cool and then chop as finely as you can. Mix with the chives.

Bring a pan of water to the boil and lower the quail's eggs in carefully. Simmer for 20 seconds, then drain and run under the cold tap briefly.

Spoon a good layer of sea salt onto a serving dish. Cut the tops off the quail's eggs to expose the yolk and stand them in the salt. Spoon the bacon mixture on top of each one and serve immediately.

To eat, knock them back like a shot, squeezing the shell slightly to release the egg.

DEEP-FRIED SALMON SKINS

Many years ago at the Dorchester we used to fry up the skins of gravadlax and smoked salmon to serve as bar snacks. Since then I've always saved skins from smoked salmon, or even fresh salmon. They really are delicious little snacks, made from something you would usually just throw away.

Serves 6–8

vegetable or corn oil for deep-frying
skin from 1–2 sides of smoked or fresh salmon

Heat an 8cm depth of oil in a deep-fat fryer or other suitable deep, heavy pan to 160–180°C. Cut the salmon skins roughly into rough strips, 2–3cm long and 1cm wide.

Deep-fry the skins a handful or so at a time, stirring them every so often, for 2–3 minutes until crisp. Drain on kitchen paper and serve just warm or cold.

DEEP-FRIED SCALLOP FRILLS

Scallop frills! You may wonder what the hell I'm on about but as usual I don't like to see good things going to waste. These are the frills surrounding the white nugget of scallop meat and they normally end up in the bin. To accumulate enough, ask your fishmonger to keep them for you, or save them up in the freezer.

Serves 6–8

200–250g scallop frills, black sac removed and well washed
salt and freshly ground black pepper
150g self-raising flour
200ml milk
vegetable or corn oil for deep-frying

Check that the scallop frills are clean and that all of the sand has been washed away, then place them in a pan, cover with water and add 1–2 tsp salt. Bring to the boil, lower the heat and simmer for 3–4 minutes, then drain in a colander and dry the frills on kitchen paper.

Season the flour well. Have 3 bowls ready, one containing the seasoned flour, one for the milk and the third for the finished scallop frills.

Heat an 8cm depth of oil in a deep-fat fryer or other suitable deep, heavy pan to 160–180°C. Coat the scallop frills in the flour, shaking off any excess, then pass them through the milk and again through the flour. Deep-fry the frills in batches, moving them around in the oil, for 2–3 minutes until golden.

Remove the scallop frills with a slotted spoon and drain on kitchen paper. Sprinkle with salt and serve.

PORK CRACKLING WITH BRAMLEY APPLE SAUCE

Pork crackling is certainly our most popular bar snack and has become a permanent fixture on the menu. I've recently started serving it with Bramley apple sauce, which helps cut the fattiness. Most butchers would be happy to part with – or sell you – some pork rind with a fat layer left on. Eat the crackling on the day you make it.

Serves 6–10

1kg pork rind, with a 5mm layer of fat left on
2–3 tbsp Cornish sea salt

For the Bramley apple sauce
1 Bramley apple
1 tbsp caster sugar

Preheat the oven to 200°C/gas mark 6. Cut the pork rind into rough strips, about 12cm long and 3cm wide. Place in a pan of cold water, bring to the boil and simmer for about 15 minutes. Drain well, place on a baking tray and scatter with 1 tbsp sea salt. Roast for about 1 hour until the rind is crisp, turning and draining the fat from the tray every so often (save it to roast potatoes).

Meanwhile, make the apple sauce. Peel, quarter and core the apple, then cut into chunks and place in a heavy-based pan over a medium heat. Add the sugar and cook for about 10 minutes, stirring every so often, until the apple has broken up. Remove from the heat. You can give the sauce a bit of a whisk to make it smoother if you wish, but I like it quite chunky. Transfer to individual serving bowls.

Drain the pork in a colander and scatter over some more salt while hot. Serve the crackling on a platter, with the apple sauce as a dip on the side.

DRINKS

It's not easy in a British focused restaurant to have a purely British drinks list. Beer, Perry and cider don't pose a problem, but there are not yet enough quality wine producers to offer an entirely British wine list that will satisfy customers needs and guarantee quality. I do, however, have a couple of great home-produced wines on the menu.

NYETIMBER Made with traditional Champagne variety grapes in West Chiltington, West Sussex, by wine maker Cherie Spriggs, this excellent sparkling wine has been compared with some of the best Champagnes in France; it's even competed successfully in international competitions.

BACCHUS CODDINGTON Another wine that has secured a place on our list. It is produced from a tiny 1½ acre vineyard near Ledbury in Herefordshire. Denis and Ann Savage planted their Bacchus grapes in 1983, so by British standards it's quite an established vineyard, albeit on a small scale. In 2008, I managed to secure the whole vintage, which amounts to about 20 cases for the restaurants.

HIX OYSTER ALE When I first opened the Oyster & Chop House, among the bottled beers I chose to sell Hugh Fearnley-Whittingstall's and Rick Stein's beers, as a nod to other West Country foodies and because they are bloody good. I later decided I'd like to do my own beer – ideally a dark ale to drink with oysters. Palmers, my local brewery in Bridport, Dorset, suggested re-branding Tally Ho which has been around since I was legally permitted to drink. It seemed just the kind of ale to offer with oysters, so Hix Oyster Ale was added to our beer selection. It proved so popular with guests that I decided to enter it for a Great Taste Award; to my surprise – like my smoked salmon – it won gold. We've also found that the ale works really well for braising beef, so it goes into our Beef and oyster pie (on page 154), which has become a signature dish at the restaurant.

SOMERSET CIDER BRANDY To my mind Julian Temperley is the best drink producer in the country. Not only has he rescued and kept going traditional cider apple varieties to produce excellent cider, but he also makes cider brandy that's on a par with some of the great Calvados produced in France. There is a single variety Kingston Black apéritif,

which is particularly good. Ever resourceful, Julian managed to rescue some of the oak barrels washed up on Branscome beach from the Napoli disaster, which he now uses to age some of his cider brandy, appropriately re-named Shipwreck. We also recently celebrated the release of his 20-year-old cider brandy. Julian's neighbour's morello cherries get steeped in his apple eau-de-vie, which we use to make our house cocktail, the Hix Fix.

TONNIX Last year Mitch Tonks and I visited one of our wine producers, Quinta de la Rosa, on the Douro in Portugal with our wine merchant John Hutton. On arrival, we were offered glasses of Sophia Sling – the winery's house cocktail of white port with Fever-Tree tonic, ice and lemon – named after Sophia Bergqvist who owns the vineyard. I'm not sure when white port last passed my lips – probably as a brief taster before marinating foie gras in it many years ago – but it tasted superb. Both Mitch and I immediately placed orders for white port for our restaurants and I added Sophia Sling to our drinks menu.

The following evening, after a tour and a picnic on the vineyard, Mitch suggested we chose a white wine from Quinta de la Rosa to serve with seafood in our restaurants. We all thought it was a great idea and late in the evening around the dinner table we came up with the name Tonnix. Tracey Emin agreed do the label for us and within about 8 weeks the wine was on sale and flying out of the restaurants. We all, including Tracey, support the RNLI so we decided that 50p per bottle should go to the charity.

HIX FIX This has become the most popular cocktail in all of the restaurants and we often serve it instead of Champagne when we do parties. It was devised when I gave Jonathan Jeffrey, our manager at the Oyster & Fish House in Lyme Regis, a jar of Julian Temperley's morello cherries steeped in his apple eau-de-vie. On my next visit to Lyme, I noticed 'Hix Fix' scribed on the window. 'So what's that then?' I asked. 'A Champagne cocktail made with those cherries,' Johnny informed me. As I glanced around the room, I noticed there was a Hix Fix on almost every table. I later bought some old-fashioned Champagne saucers, 'Marie Antoinette 32B cups' and the Hix Fix took off. Keith Floyd enjoyed a couple before his last lunch at the Oyster & Fish House shortly before he sadly passed away.

STARTERS

I like to give customers the feeling that the minute they set eyes on the menu they know exactly what time of the year it is. The starter menu, in particular, lends itself perfectly to adapting with the seasons.

Starters are a great platform for celebratory ingredients, such as our homegrown asparagus, which I always feature strongly. Indeed I think nothing of having four asparagus dishes on the menu during the vegetable's short late-spring/early summer season. Fortunately, the season isn't quite as short as it used to be, now that our asparagus growers are doing their utmost to bring their crops on earlier and stretch them out a bit at the other end of the season.

Gull's eggs are one of my favourite ingredients and, like asparagus, they herald the arrival of spring. They featured on our opening menu in April 2008 along with asparagus and elvers. Another popular inclusion on the starter menu is my home-cured smoked salmon (see page 46). At the height of the summer, tomatoes have a well-deserved place on the menu. Heritage tomatoes served with lovage leaves and rapeseed oil, or with little nuggets of goat's cheese and pickled walnuts, make a perfect summer first course.

Many of our starters are given seasonal tweaks through the year. Fried duck's eggs, for example, are topped with anything from tiny sprue asparagus spears and broad beans to duck livers, black pudding and spider crab. Introducing seasonal ingredients in this manner keeps the menu fresh and appealing.

SHAVED ASPARAGUS AND FENNEL WITH AGED CAERPHILLY

Slicing freshly picked asparagus into thin slivers and eating it raw may not seem the obvious way to serve this delicious vegetable, but combined with just a few other simple ingredients it works a treat. Julian Biggs, my right-hand man, came up with this little gem of a salad last year. Choose thicker stems of asparagus as they are easier to shave.

Serves 4

4–6 thick or 8–10 medium very fresh asparagus spears

1 young head of fennel, trimmed, a few feathery tops reserved

a handful of small salad leaves, such as buckler leaf sorrel, land cress etc.

salt and freshly ground black pepper

70–80g good-quality aged Caerphilly cheese, such as Gorwydd

For the dressing

grated zest and juice of ½ lemon

4–5 tbsp cold-pressed rapeseed oil

Cut off the woody ends of the asparagus and peel the lower end of the stalks. Using a mandolin or very sharp knife, cut the asparagus on the diagonal into very fine slices.

Halve the fennel and, again, using a mandolin or very sharp knife, slice the fennel as thinly as possible and place in a bowl with the asparagus.

Shake the ingredients for the dressing together in a screw-topped jar and season with salt and pepper to taste.

Add the leaves and feathery fennel tops to the asparagus and fennel and season lightly. Toss with the dressing and arrange on plates. Shave the cheese with a small, sharp knife or a vegetable peeler and scatter over the salad.

COBB EGG

Seldon, my chef at the Oyster & Fish House in Lyme Regis, developed this dish as a fishy take on a Scotch egg. Customers really took to it, as the soft yolk ran down their chins while they were overlooking the Cobb. You could make little ones with quail's eggs for bar snacks or pre-dinner drinks.

Makes 4

205g white fish fillets, such as whiting, pollack or haddock

150g sea salt flakes or rock salt crystals

4 duck's eggs

100g smoked pollack or haddock fillet, boned and skinned

freshly ground white pepper

2–3 tbsp plain flour, plus extra for dusting

1 free-range egg, beaten

60–70g fresh white breadcrumbs

vegetable or corn oil for deep-frying

Lay the white fish on a non-reactive tray, scatter over the salt and let stand for 1 hour. Rinse well under cold water, drain and pat dry.

Bring a pan of water to the boil and carefully drop in the duck's eggs, using a slotted spoon. Simmer for 5 minutes, then drain and refresh under the cold tap for several minutes to stop them cooking.

Meanwhile, check the white and smoked fish for small bones, removing any with tweezers, then put into a food processor. Pulse together to a coarse texture and season with white pepper. Divide the fish mixture into 4 portions, shape into balls and flatten them on a lightly floured surface.

Carefully shell the duck's eggs, then mould the fish mixture around them ensuring they are well sealed.

Have 3 shallow bowls ready, one containing the flour, one with the egg and the third with the breadcrumbs. One at a time, coat the duck's eggs with the flour first, shaking off any excess, then put through the beaten egg and finally into the breadcrumbs, turning them to coat all over and re-moulding as necessary.

Heat an 8cm depth of oil in a deep-fat fryer or other suitable deep, heavy pan to 140–150°C. Deep-fry the eggs for 4–5 minutes, turning them every so often to colour evenly. Remove with a slotted spoon and drain on kitchen paper.

Serve the Cobb eggs hot or warm, with salad and a herb mayonnaise or tartare sauce.

OVEN-ROASTED GARLIC-STUDDED CEPS

When ceps are in season during the autumn, there is nothing better than a plate of them simply roasted as a starter – or even as a side or vegetarian main course. I served this dish as a main course for everyone at dinner when a couple of my guests were vegetarian and I wanted a dish that would satisfy everyone. It went down a treat.

Serves 4

1kg firm medium ceps
6–8 garlic cloves, peeled and sliced
200g butter
salt and freshly ground black pepper
2 tbsp chopped parsley

Preheat the oven to 220°C/gas mark 7. Clean the ceps with a cloth and make about 5 incisions in each one with the point of a knife. Push a slice of garlic into each incision.

Melt half of the butter in a roasting tray. Add the ceps, turn to coat them in the butter and season generously with salt and pepper. Roast in the oven for 20–30 minutes until the ceps are just tender, turning them every so often to ensure they cook and colour evenly.

Add the rest of the butter and the chopped parsley, stir well and return to the oven for 2–3 minutes. Serve at once.

FRIED DUCK'S EGG WITH SPIDER CRAB AND SEA GREENS

There are lots of interesting things you can serve with a fried duck's egg. Spider crab, which is sadly underused in this country, and a few handfuls of sea vegetables give this dish a taste of the sea. Vary the vegetables according to what you are able to gather, or, if you haven't got foraging tendencies, buy samphire in season.

Serves 4

1 small-medium spider crab, cooked

3–4 tbsp cold-pressed rapeseed oil

a few handfuls of wild sea vegetables, such as samphire, sea purslane, small sea beet leaves

4 duck's eggs

sea salt and freshly ground black pepper

a couple of generous knobs of butter

Remove the brown meat from the spider crab body shell and set aside. Crack open the claws, quarter the inner body shell and remove as much white meat as possible. Put the brown meat into a blender with 2 tbsp rapeseed oil and blend until smooth. It should be a pouring consistency; if not add a little water.

Trim the sea vegetables of any woody stalks and wash them well. Bring a pan of water to the boil, add the sea vegetables and blanch for about 30 seconds, then drain.

Heat 1–2 tbsp rapeseed oil in a frying pan and fry the duck's eggs gently for a couple of minutes, lightly seasoning the whites.

Meanwhile, heat the butter in a pan and toss in the sea vegetables and white crab meat. Warm through briefly and season lightly.

Transfer the eggs to warmed plates, scatter the sea vegetables and crab over the egg white and spoon a little of the brown meat sauce around. Grind some pepper and salt over the yolks and serve at once.

CUTTLEFISH WITH SEA ASTER

I can't understand why we don't eat more cuttlefish in the UK; our fishermen land loads of the stuff but it all goes off to Spain and France. The season runs from midwinter through until June, when you can gather sea aster – a long-leafed green sea vegetable with a fragrant flavour.

Serves 4

80g butter
1 small onion, peeled and finely chopped
4 garlic cloves, peeled and crushed
½ tbsp plain flour
100ml white wine
250ml fish stock
1 bay leaf
salt and freshly ground black pepper
450–500g cleaned cuttlefish
1 tbsp vegetable or cold-pressed rapeseed oil
4 sachets (30g) cuttlefish ink
2 tbsp double cream
2 handfuls of sea aster, washed and dried

Melt half of the butter in a heavy-based saucepan and add the onion and garlic. Cook gently for 3–4 minutes, stirring every so often. Add the flour and stir over a low heat for 20 seconds, then gradually whisk in the wine and fish stock, keeping the sauce smooth. Add the bay leaf, season and simmer gently for about 20 minutes.

Cut the cuttlefish roughly into 3cm squares and season. Heat the oil in a heavy-based frying pan and fry the cuttlefish over a high heat, stirring occasionally, for a few minutes to colour lightly. Drain on kitchen paper. Add the cuttlefish to the sauce along with the ink and simmer gently for about 10 minutes until it is tender. Add the cream, re-season and simmer for a minute or two.

Melt the rest of the butter in a heavy-based pan and cook the sea aster for a minute or so until wilted. To serve, spoon the cuttlefish and sauce into a bowl and spoon over the sea aster.

MANX QUEENIES WITH CUCUMBER AND WILD FENNEL

Last year I was invited to the Isle of Man Queenie Festival, the first to be held. As you might guess, fishing for queen scallops is a pretty serious business on the island. Given that it takes as long to prep a little queenie as it does to clean a large scallop, you could argue that it's not worthwhile, but they are delicious and the possibilities are endless. Very fresh queenies are excellent eaten raw – I rate them on a par with oysters and they can be served in the same way.

Serves 4

24–32 very fresh queenies, prepared and left in the half-shell

For the dressing
2 shallots, peeled and finely chopped
2 tbsp cider vinegar
⅓ cucumber
1 tbsp cold-pressed rapeseed oil
½ tbsp chopped wild fennel
juice of ½ lemon
salt and freshly ground black pepper

For the dressing, place the shallots and cider vinegar in a small pan, bring to the boil, then tip into a bowl.

Cut the cucumber in half lengthways and scoop out the seeds with a teaspoon. Finely chop the cucumber into 5mm dice, then add to the shallots. Add the rapeseed oil, fennel and lemon juice, toss to combine and season well. Leave to stand for about 20 minutes.

Spoon the marinated cucumber onto the queenies and serve.

DE BEAUVOIR SMOKED SALMON – HIX CURE

Before we opened the Oyster & Chop House, I decided that I needed to have something on the menu that would stand out as an artisan dish. I had recently come across a smoker by Bradley, an American company, and started playing around with cold-smoked salmon.

I asked Richard Cook at the Severn and Wye smokery for a bit of friendly advice on curing and settled on a mix of industrial rock salt and molasses sugar – dry curing the fish, rather as you would to make a gravadlax. From Bradley's range of smoking bisquettes I opted for a mix of oak and apple wood. On my first attempt I liked the flavour so much that I haven't bothered to experiment with any other options since.

Admittedly, early on I did have a few disasters with my cold-smoking, resulting in a number of hot-smoked trials as the heat of the smoking element gradually cooked the fish. However, installing a metre length of galvanised ducting between the smoke generator and the cabinet containing the fish fillets solved the problem.

The provenance of the fish was, of course, important. As Lloch Duart freedom food salmon was already on the menu, I used fillets from the smaller fish that were delivered from day one. I've tweaked the smoking times along the way; the smoking cabinet is quite small – the size of a small domestic fridge – so the salmon needs less time than it would in a large-scale commercial smoker. Generally, I leave the fish in for 5 or 6 hours, or overnight depending what time I go to bed, that is…

Smoking your own salmon certainly makes you appreciate what a real artisan smoker does, although these days most of our smoke houses are electronically operated by a computerised system. There are, however, still a few around that operate in the old-fashioned way.

Believe it or not, I smoke my fish in my back garden in De Beauvoir, Hackney. Initially the neighbours were quite suspicious about me carrying salmon to the bottom of the garden with my fishing headlamp on. But they do like the salmon and the smoker itself doesn't actually give out much smoke – no more than a few people having a fag at the bottom of the garden.

From the beginning I sliced the salmon Scandinavian-style, almost vertically, cutting it into slices about 3mm thick. This way you really get to taste the fish and enjoy the smoky flavour, which is rarely possible with the ubiquitous paper-thin slices that you can see the plate through.

Not only has my smoked salmon become very popular with our restaurant customers, fellow chefs have shown an interest, too. Even my mate Richard Corrigan now has it on his menu.

MUTTON SCRUMPETS WITH WILD GARLIC MAYONNAISE

This is a lovely old-fashioned dish, which makes good use of tasty breast of lamb or mutton, an underused and inexpensive cut. It makes a great starter or snack to share, accompanied by a wild garlic mayonnaise.

Serves 4

300–400g boneless breast of mutton or lamb
salt and freshly ground black pepper
1 head of garlic, halved and roughly chopped
a few sprigs each of rosemary and thyme
2–3 tbsp plain flour
2 free-range medium eggs, beaten
60–70g fresh white breadcrumbs
vegetable or corn oil for deep-frying
2–3 tbsp mayonnaise (see page 28)
1 tbsp wild garlic purée (see page 132), or chopped garlic chives
1 lemon, quartered, to serve

Preheat the oven to 160°C/gas mark 3. Place the mutton in an ovenproof dish (with a tight-fitting lid). Season well and scatter over the chopped garlic and herbs. Cover and cook in the oven for 2 hours or until very tender, basting regularly and turning the oven down if necessary. Leave to cool overnight.

Scrape away any fat residue from the mutton and any fat that hasn't rendered down during cooking. Cut the breast into 1cm wide strips, 3–4cm long.

Have 3 bowls ready, one with the flour, one with the eggs and the third with the breadcrumbs. Season the flour. Heat a 6cm depth of oil in a deep-fat fryer or other suitable deep, heavy pan to 160–180°C.

Mix the mayonnaise with the wild garlic purée or garlic chives.

Pass the mutton strips through the seasoned flour, shaking off excess, then through the egg and finally coat in the breadcrumbs. Deep-fry the strips in batches for 2–3 minutes, moving them around in the oil until golden and crisp. Lift out with a slotted spoon and drain on kitchen paper.

Serve the mutton scrumpets with lemon wedges and the wild garlic mayonnaise on the side.

MACKEREL WITH BROAD BEANS AND ARTICHOKES

Mackerel is such a versatile fish, but it is rarely treated in an interesting way, which is a great shame. With this recipe, you can pack the mackerel immersed in the spiced oil in kilner jars and keep it in the fridge for a week or so to have as a quick, tasty snack. Here I'm serving it as a summery salad with artichokes. This is the kind of salad that you might have in the south of France but it uses British ingredients – our artichokes are from Somerset.

Serves 4

6 medium mackerel, filleted
100ml cold-pressed rapeseed oil
2 large shallots, peeled and finely chopped
6 garlic cloves, peeled and sliced
1 small, medium-strength chilli, stalk removed and finely chopped
12 black peppercorns, lightly crushed
1 tsp fennel seeds, crushed
½ tsp ground cumin
1 tbsp cider vinegar
juice of ½ lemon
Cornish sea salt

For the artichokes and beans
2 large globe artichokes
juice of ½ lemon
200g podded broad beans

To serve
1 tbsp roughly chopped parsley

Have the mackerel fillets ready. Heat 2 tbsp rapeseed oil in a saucepan and add the shallots and garlic with the chilli, crushed pepper and spices. Cook gently for 2–3 minutes until soft, without colouring.

Add the cider vinegar, lemon juice and remaining oil. Bring to a gentle simmer, season well with salt and drop in the mackerel fillets. Bring back to a simmer, take off the heat, cover and leave to cool.

Meanwhile, prepare the artichokes one at a time. Have ready a bowl of cold water with the lemon juice added. Cut off the stem from the artichoke and carefully cut away the leaves with a serrated knife until the meaty heart is exposed; try to keep the circular shape. Using a spoon, scoop out the hairy choke, leaving the heart. Immerse the artichoke in the lemon water to prevent discoloration.

Put the artichoke hearts in a non-reactive saucepan with the lemon water, add a good pinch of salt and bring to the boil. Lower the heat and simmer for about 12–15 minutes until the artichokes are tender, then leave to cool in the liquid.

Bring a pan of salted water to the boil. Add the broad beans and cook for 3–4 minutes until tender, then drain and run briefly under the cold tap. Remove the tough skins from larger beans; leave smaller ones as they are.

When ready to serve, cut each artichoke heart into 8 wedges. Remove the mackerel from the oil with a slotted spoon and break the fillets into 4 or 5 pieces. Mix the broad beans and artichokes with a few spoonfuls of the mackerel liquor and season. Divide among plates and arrange the mackerel on top. Spoon over some more dressing and scatter over the chopped parsley.

HEAVEN AND EARTH

This is based upon *himmel und erder,* a popular German dish. According to my mate, Steve Claydon, who is a huge fan, the soft, silky black pudding is the heaven (*himmel*) upon the earth (*erder*) of crushed up apples and potatoes. Until recently the closest I could find to the German soft black pudding was Spanish morcilla, which works pretty well. Then Peter Gott of Sillfield Farm in the Lake District kindly developed a soft version of his black pudding for me, which is perfect. You can buy it from Borough Market, though you may well have a local butcher who makes something similar and you can soften it up as suggested if necessary. Wrapping the pudding in pig's caul stops it bursting during cooking.

Serves 4

300–400g good-quality soft black pudding
about 100ml chicken stock (if needed)
about 100g caul fat, rinsed
300g potatoes (for mashing), peeled and quartered
salt and freshly ground black pepper
1 cooking apple
½ tbsp caster sugar
about 120g butter

Unless your black pudding is already soft, place it in a bowl and mix in enough stock to give a soft but not wet consistency. Spread the caul fat out on a work surface and pat dry with kitchen paper. Shape the black pudding into 4 balls and cut a piece of caul large enough to wrap around each one. Wrap securely and overlap slightly. If the caul is very thin, add another layer.

Simmer the potatoes in a pan of salted water until just tender. Meanwhile, peel, quarter and core the apple, then cut into chunks and place in a saucepan with the sugar. Cook over a low heat, stirring every so often, until soft and almost falling apart.

Drain the cooked potatoes and return to a low heat for 30 seconds or so to dry out. Crush lightly with a fork or potato masher, season and stir in the apple and half of the butter; keep warm.

Preheat the grill to medium. Melt the remaining butter. Place the black pudding parcels on a grill tray and brush with melted butter. Grill for 6–7 minutes until evenly browned, turning and basting with more butter during cooking.

To serve, spoon the apple and potato into the centre of each warmed plate and flatten slightly with the back of a spoon. Place the black pudding in the middle and serve at once.

SALADS

Salads are a crucial part of a menu whether they are a simple side dish or a more complex starter featuring a seasonal ingredient. Our menu at the Oyster & Chop House may seem a bit masculine on the surface, but within we balance it up with some lighter options, according to what's in season.

A salad should always be very fresh and full of flavour. A good combination of just a few, flavourful leaves really does set aside a first-rate salad from a bog-standard one based on boring supermarket packs of ready-washed salad leaves. I keep a nice selection of leaves growing in the garden, such as buckler leaf or silver sorrel, parcel (leaf celery), parsley, rocket, purslane and land cress, and I encourage edible weeds like bittercress and chickweed to grow, instead of tossing them into the compost bin or spraying weedkiller on them.

Many edible decorative plants, including nasturtiums and amaranth, also make a good addition to the salad bowl along with some freshly cut common garden herbs like chervil, flat-leaf parsley and small-leafed Greek basil. On their own, a good selection of these leaves makes a memorable salad. Add seasonal ingredients like asparagus, game or fish, and you start to realise that a salad can be really exhilarating.

If you are serving a side salad, just one or two distinctive leaves can often be more pleasing than a complicated mix of several ingredients. Native leaves, such as watercress, Cos lettuce or Little Gem hearts, old-fashioned English round or Webb's lettuce, pea shoots and tendrils are perfect choices for a simple side salad or starter.

DRESSINGS

A good salad, apart from having great tasty leaves, is about the dressing. Good salad leaves deserve to be well dressed and I like to have a range of vinegars and oils so I can make a bespoke dressing to suit the ingredients in the salad and the occasion. Other flavourings can be added to round off the dressing and match it to the food you are serving the salad with. Mustard is the obvious choice – there are lots of different types – but horseradish works well or you can even add fruit as I do for my Bramble dressing.

PICKLED WALNUT DRESSING

Pickled walnuts are one of those old-fashioned, almost forgotten British condiments. Their sweet, acidic taste works brilliantly in a dressing. This one goes really well with beetroot or cheese-based salads, though once you've tasted it you'll probably want to put it on everything.

Serves 4–6

2–3 good-quality pickled walnuts, chopped, plus 2 tbsp of their juice
4–5 tbsp cold-pressed rapeseed oil
salt and freshly ground black pepper

Whisk all of the ingredients together in a bowl or shake in a screw-topped jar or bottle, seasoning with salt and pepper to taste.

BRAMBLE DRESSING

The lovely deep mauve colour and the combination of sweet and acidic flavours makes this dressing the perfect match for game salads. I haven't used much in the way of fruity dressings since the eighties, but this one makes great use of an abundant supply of wild blackberries.

Serves 4–6

6–8 blackberries
1 tbsp cider vinegar
4 tbsp cold-pressed rapeseed oil
salt and freshly ground black pepper

Crush the blackberries in a bowl using a fork, then whisk in the cider vinegar and rapeseed oil. Season with salt and pepper to taste. Leave to stand for about 30 minutes, then push through a sieve with the back of a spoon into a bowl and re-season the dressing if necessary.

TEWKESBURY MUSTARD DRESSING

Tewkesbury mustard is a blend of mustard and horseradish with a clean taste and sharp bite, which dates back to Shakespearian times. It's perfect to use in place of Dijon mustard in dressings to give a truly British taste.

Serves 4–6

1 tbsp cider vinegar
1 tbsp Tewkesbury mustard
4 tbsp cold-pressed rapeseed oil
salt and freshly ground black pepper

Whisk the cider vinegar, mustard and rapeseed oil together in a bowl or shake in a screw-topped jar or bottle. Season the dressing with salt and pepper to taste.

HONEY AND MUSTARD DRESSING

This is a great dressing for slightly bitter leaves like dandelion or chicory, or to go with a ham hock salad.

Serves 4–6

2 tbsp cider vinegar
1 tbsp clear honey
1 tbsp wholegrain mustard
3 tbsp cold-pressed rapeseed oil
2–3 tbsp vegetable or corn oil
salt and freshly ground black pepper

Whisk the cider vinegar, honey, mustard and oils together in a bowl or shake in a screw-topped jar or bottle. Season with salt and pepper to taste.

MIMOSA DRESSING

We developed this dressing years ago – for the classic salad that is topped with grated egg to give the look of a mimosa flower. Very rarely do we make the actual dish but we use the dressing in many other salads.

Serves 4–6

½ tbsp cider vinegar
juice of ½ small lemon
1 garlic clove, peeled and halved
2 sprigs of tarragon
2 tbsp vegetable or corn oil
2–3 tbsp cold-pressed rapeseed oil
salt and freshly ground black pepper

Whisk the cider vinegar, lemon juice, garlic, tarragon and oils together or shake in a screw-topped jar or bottle. Season with salt and pepper to taste. Leave to infuse overnight and strain before using.

BLUE CHEESE DRESSING

This is a useful way to use up little bits of blue cheese and can transform a salad into something rather special. It is ideal with robust leaves like Little Gem lettuce and chicory, but I wouldn't try it on more delicate leaves as it will overpower them.

Serves 4–6

1 tbsp cider vinegar
½ tsp Tewkesbury mustard
20g blue cheese
2 tbsp cold-pressed rapeseed oil
2 tbsp vegetable or corn oil
salt and freshly ground black pepper

Blend the cider vinegar, mustard, blue cheese and oils together in a blender and season with salt and pepper to taste. If the dressing is too thick, thin it with a little water.

ASPARAGUS AND SORREL SALAD

Sprue asparagus, the little offshoots from the asparagus plant, aren't that exciting to eat on their own dunked into hollandaise, but they do make a great salad. Here I've combined them with buckler leaf or silver sorrel, which is one of my favourite little salad leaves. You can easily transform this simple side salad into a starter or lunch dish by topping it with a deep-fried duck's egg (see below).

Serves 4

250g sprue asparagus spears, trimmed

salt and freshly ground black pepper

a couple of handfuls of buckler leaf sorrel or other small tasty leaves, washed and dried

Mimosa dressing (see page 55)

Add the asparagus to a pan of boiling salted water and cook for 2–3 minutes until tender, then drain and briefly refresh under the cold tap. Cut each spear into 2 or 3 pieces.

Arrange the sorrel leaves and asparagus on plates, season and spoon over the dressing.

Variation

Boil 4 eggs as for Cobb egg (page 40), then coat directly with flour, egg and breadcrumbs (omitting the fish paste). Deep-fry for 2–3 minutes only, then drain on kitchen paper. Cut the eggs in half and serve on top of the salad.

FENNEL SALAD

Fennel is an underused vegetable in this country, though it has many possibilities – both raw and cooked. Try serving this salad with marinated or smoked fish. You could also combine it with thinly sliced cucumber (that has been halved lengthways and deseeded) for a light summery garnish to grilled fish.

Serves 4

2 young fennel bulbs, trimmed and green tops reserved

2–3 tbsp cider vinegar

sea salt and freshly ground white pepper

2–3 tbsp cold-pressed rapeseed oil

Halve the fennel bulbs and slice them as thinly as possible, using a mandolin or very sharp knife. Tip into a bowl, add the cider vinegar and season to taste. Toss to mix and leave for about an hour, stirring every so often.

Chop the green fennel tops and add to the fennel with the rapeseed oil. Toss to combine, then taste and adjust the seasoning if necessary. Serve within a couple of hours.

BROAD BEAN, PEA AND GIROLLE SALAD

This is a really simple, fresh-tasting salad – one of those dishes that you just take one look at and know it's summer. You can vary the beans if you wish, perhaps adding some runners or bobby beans.

Serves 4

1 garlic clove, peeled and sliced

4 tbsp cold-pressed rapeseed oil

a few sprigs of tarragon, leaves removed and stalks reserved

sea salt and freshly ground black pepper

200–250g girolles, cleaned

200g podded peas

200g podded broad beans

a pinch of caster sugar

1 tbsp cider vinegar

a handful of pea shoots (if available)

Put the garlic, rapeseed oil and tarragon stalks into a wide saucepan with about 3 tbsp water. Season well and bring to the boil. Add the girolles, cover with a lid and cook over a low heat for 3–4 minutes, turning them with a spoon every so often. Take off the heat, remove the lid and leave to cool a little.

Cook the peas and broad beans separately in boiling salted water for a few minutes until just tender, adding a little caster sugar to the cooking water for the peas. Drain and remove the tough skins from any larger broad beans; leave small ones as they are.

Remove the girolles from their liquid with a slotted spoon and set aside on a plate.

To make the dressing, carefully pour off the oily part of the girolle cooking liquid into a bowl, leaving the watery liquid behind in the pan. Whisk the cider vinegar into the oil. Chop the tarragon leaves and stir these in, too. Check the seasoning.

Toss the peas and broad beans in the dressing, then spoon onto serving plates. Scatter the girolles on top, along with a few pea shoots, if using. Spoon a little more dressing over the salad and serve.

POTATO SALAD WITH BACON AND SPRING ONIONS

I discovered this great warm potato salad years ago while working at the Dorchester. It goes with just about anything – from sausages to a piece of grilled salmon – or you can serve it as part of a buffet salad selection. You could use other waxy potatoes, such as Charlotte or Pink Fir Apple.

Serves 4–6

300–350g Anya or other waxy potatoes (unpeeled)

sea salt and freshly ground black pepper

1 medium onion, peeled and finely chopped

3 rashers of rindless streaky bacon, finely chopped

1 tsp cumin seeds

3 tbsp cider vinegar

250ml chicken stock

3–4 tbsp cold-pressed rapeseed oil

4 spring onions, trimmed and finely chopped

Cook the potatoes in a pan of boiling salted water for 12–15 minutes until just tender. Drain and leave until cool enough to handle.

Meanwhile, put the onion, bacon, cumin seeds, cider vinegar and chicken stock into a saucepan and simmer gently until the liquid has reduced by about two-thirds, then take off the heat.

Peel the potatoes and cut into 3mm thick slices. Add to the onion and bacon mixture, along with the rapeseed oil. Toss gently to mix and season with salt and pepper to taste.

Cover and leave to stand for up to an hour until ready to serve, giving an occasional stir to encourage the potatoes to absorb all the flavours. Just before serving, add the spring onions and toss gently.

TOMATO SALAD WITH LANCASHIRE CHEESE AND PICKLED WALNUTS

A number of tomato growers in this country are growing some great heritage varieties, which make a really interesting salad. Pickled walnuts, with their sweet vinegary flavour, really do complement the tomatoes. Try to find a good aged Lancashire or Cheddar, which gives a nice natural seasoning to the salad.

Serves 4

400–450g mixed ripe flavourful tomatoes
2–3 pickled walnuts, plus 1–2 tbsp of their juice
3–4 tbsp cold-pressed rapeseed oil
salt and freshly ground black pepper
100g aged Lancashire or Cheddar cheese

Cut the tomatoes into fairly even-sized wedges and chunks, either halving small cherry tomatoes or leaving them whole.

Chop the pickled walnuts into small pieces and mix in a bowl with some of their juice and the rapeseed oil. Season with salt and pepper to taste.

Arrange the tomatoes on individual plates or one large serving platter and spoon over the pickled walnut dressing. Shave the cheese into thin slices with a sharp knife or vegetable peeler and scatter over the tomatoes.

BLUE MONDAY SALAD

Blue Monday, created by the Evenlode Partnership (see page 186), has become my favourite British blue cheese. You can serve this salad as a starter or side dish, but bear in mind the intensity of the dressing for the rest of the meal. If you can't get hold of cobnuts, substitute walnuts or hazelnuts. Use Blue Monday in the dressing, too, if you can get it.

Serves 4

25–30 cobnuts, shelled
½ tbsp cold-pressed rapeseed oil
2–3 tsp Cornish sea salt
4 small Little Gem lettuce, washed and dried
Blue cheese dressing (page 55)
50–60g Blue Monday, or other blue cheese

Heat the grill to medium. Place the cobnuts on a grill tray and mix with the rapeseed oil and salt. Grill until lightly toasted, then leave to cool.

Toss the salad leaves in the dressing and arrange on serving plates or bowls. Break the cheese into pieces and scatter over the top of the salad, along with the toasted cobnuts.

SEASHORE SALAD

We developed this salad at the Oyster & Fish House in Lyme Regis, making good use of the diverse seafood and seashore vegetables available along the Dorset coast. It occasionally appears on the menu in Smithfield and is a reminder of the great seafood we have in our coastal waters. You can really use whatever seafood and seashore vegetables you can get your hands on. When rock samphire is around, we pickle it and use it to add a little acidity to the salad, but you could use capers in much the same way.

Serves 4

150–200g cockles or surf clams, cleaned
150–200g mussels, cleaned
50ml white wine
4 medium scallops, shelled and cleaned
a couple of handfuls of sea vegetables, such as small leaves of sea beet, samphire, sea purslane, sea aster and wild fennel, trimmed of woody stalks and washed
2–3 tbsp freshly picked white crab meat
other seafood, such as cooked lobster, prawns etc. (optional)
4 oysters, shucked and left in the half-shell

For the dressing
juice of ½ lemon
1 tbsp cider vinegar
4–5 tbsp cold-pressed rapeseed oil
sea salt and freshly ground black pepper

Put the cockles and mussels in a pan with the white wine. Cover with a tight-fitting lid and cook over a high heat for 3–4 minutes, shaking the pan every so often until they open. Tip into a colander, reserving the juices; discard any molluscs that remain closed.

Strain the liquor through a fine-meshed sieve into a small saucepan and bring to the boil. Halve the scallops, lay in a small dish and pour the hot liquid over them; leave to cool.

Bring a pan of lightly salted water to the boil and blanch whichever sea vegetable you are using for 20 seconds, then refresh under the cold tap.

For the dressing, whisk the lemon juice, cider vinegar and rapeseed oil together with a little of the liquid from the scallops and season to taste.

To serve, remove half of the mussels and cockles from their shells. Arrange together with the sea vegetable(s) and the rest of the shellfish, except the oysters, on individual plates or one large platter. Spoon over the dressing and sit the oysters on top.

FISH HOUSE SALAD

This is my British take on a *salade Niçoise*, using fresh mackerel in place of the typical tinned tuna. Cooking the mackerel in oil in the way I have here gives a flavour that is comparable to tinned tuna, but better in my view and, of course, it's a much more sustainable option.

Serves 4–6

about 150ml cold-pressed rapeseed oil

1 small onion, peeled and finely chopped

2 garlic cloves, peeled and sliced

1 red chilli, halved and deseeded

½ tsp cumin seeds

a few sprigs of thyme

2 tbsp cider vinegar, plus a little extra for the dressing

juice of ½ lemon

salt and freshly ground black pepper

4 medium or 8 small mackerel fillets

12–16 new potatoes (unpeeled)

80–100g green beans

100–120g podded broad beans

4 free-range medium eggs

200–250g ripe tomatoes (mixed or 1 variety)

2 Little Gem lettuces, washed and dried

Heat 3 tbsp of the rapeseed oil in a saucepan and gently cook the onion and garlic with the chilli, cumin and thyme for 2–3 minutes, without colouring, until soft. Add all but 1 tbsp of the remaining rapeseed oil with the cider vinegar and lemon juice. Bring to a gentle simmer and season well with sea salt.

Meanwhile, lightly season the mackerel fillets with salt and pepper and heat 1 tbsp rapeseed oil in a non-stick frying pan. Fry the mackerel fillets, skin side down first, over a high heat, for 2–3 minutes on each side. Now immerse the mackerel fillets in the flavoured oil and leave to cool.

Add the potatoes to a pan of salted water, bring to the boil and cook for 12–15 minutes until just tender. Drain and leave until cool enough to handle, then halve or quarter them.

Cook the green beans and broad beans separately in boiling salted water until just tender, then drain and refresh under cold water. Remove the skins from any larger broad beans.

Bring a pan of water to the boil and carefully drop in the eggs, using a slotted spoon. Simmer for 5 minutes, then drain and refresh under the cold tap. Shell the eggs and halve or quarter them.

Remove the mackerel from the oil with a slotted spoon and set aside. For the dressing, strain the flavoured oil through a fine-meshed sieve into a bowl. Whisk well and add a little more cider vinegar to taste.

To serve, cut the tomatoes into wedges or chunks. Toss the lettuce leaves with the green beans, broad beans, potatoes, tomatoes and some of the dressing. Season, then arrange in serving bowls. Break the mackerel into chunks and arrange on top of the leaves with the eggs. Spoon over some more dressing and serve.

GROUSE SALAD WITH PARSNIP CRISPS AND BRAMBLE DRESSING

When you have a game bird with a high price tag, like grouse, it's important to get the most out of your bird. I'm a big fan of traditional roast grouse with all the trimmings and I rarely go off piste, but there are a couple of dishes that I will knock up during the season so customers can have grouse as a starter and something else for the main course. A salad is a lovely light option; on toast is another of my favourites - spread the livers on toast and scatter with wild mushrooms. What's more if you use the breasts for a starter you can get yet another meal out of the bird in the form of a soup (see page 80).

Serves 4

2 oven-ready grouse
2 small parsnips, scrubbed clean
vegetable or corn oil for deep-frying
sea salt and freshly ground black pepper
a couple of knobs of butter, softened
4 rashers of streaky bacon, cut into 1cm pieces
a couple of handfuls of small flavoursome salad leaves and herbs
Bramble dressing (page 54)

Preheat the oven to 240°C/gas mark 9 and have the grouse ready at room temperature. Top and tail the parsnips, leaving the skin on unless it is very brown. Using a sharp mandolin or vegetable peeler, slice them lengthways as thinly as possible, rinse well and then pat dry with a clean tea towel. Heat about an 8cm depth of oil in a deep-fat fryer or other suitable deep, heavy pan to 180°C.

Fry the parsnip slices in the hot oil in small batches, stirring to ensure that they don't stick together. The parsnip slices will take a while to colour (avoid over-browning them) and even then may still appear soft (they will crisp up on drying). Remove with a slotted spoon, drain on kitchen paper and sprinkle with salt. Leave them to dry somewhere warm but not hot.

Season the grouse with salt and pepper and rub the breasts with butter. Roast for about 15 minutes, keeping them nice and pink, then set aside to rest in a warm spot. Meanwhile, fry the bacon pieces in a dry pan for a few minutes until crisp.

To serve, carefully remove the grouse breasts from the carcass and cut each one into 6 or 7 slices. Arrange the leaves on individual plates with the grouse and bacon. Spoon over the bramble dressing, then scatter or pile the parsnip crisps on top.

SALT BEEF AND GREEN SPLIT GREEN SALAD

The old London tradition of salt beef sandwiches carries on in a few bagel shops and sandwich bars around London, but salt beef can be used in other interesting ways. Brisket and silverside are the most common beef cuts to be sold salted, but my favourite is ox cheeks. You may find these tricky to get hold of, but brisket gives a similar result for this dish.

I adapt this salad throughout the year, using fresh peas in the summer, for example. I also make it with green beans – tossing them with the salt beef and using a little more mustard in the dressing.

Serves 4

500g piece salted beef brisket or ox cheeks, soaked overnight in cold water

1 onion, peeled and halved

2 celery sticks, each cut into thirds

12 black peppercorns

1 bay leaf

100g green split peas, soaked overnight in cold water

1 large shallot, peeled and finely chopped

2 tsp English mustard

1 tbsp cider vinegar

3–4 tbsp cold-pressed rapeseed oil, plus a little extra to finish

salt and freshly ground black pepper

1 large carrot, peeled and cut into thin matchsticks

a small handful of wild salad leaves, such as bittercress, chickweed and wood sorrel

Drain and rinse the salt beef and put into a saucepan with the onion, celery, peppercorns and bay leaf. Add plenty of cold water to cover, bring to the boil and skim off the scum from the surface. Lower the heat, cover and simmer very gently for about 2 hours until the beef is very tender.

About halfway through cooking the beef, drain the split peas and put them into another pan. Strain several ladlefuls of the beef cooking liquor over the peas, to cover them generously, and top up the water in the beef pan as necessary to keep the beef covered. Bring the split peas to the boil, lower the heat and simmer for about 15–20 minutes until just tender. Drain and allow to cool.

When the beef is cooked, remove from the heat and leave it to cool in the liquor.

Once the split peas have cooled, toss them in a bowl with the shallot, mustard and cider vinegar, then mix in enough rapeseed oil to make a thick dressing. Season with salt and pepper to taste.

To serve, spoon the split peas onto serving plates and spread them out a little with the back of the spoon. Cut the beef into smallish chunks or coarsely shred it and mix with a little rapeseed oil. Pile the beef on top of the split peas, then scatter the carrot and a few salad leaves over the top.

SOUPS

The quality of the soups on a menu is a good test of any restaurant. I find that the effort that goes into producing a starter, main or dessert is often not matched with a soup. When you've gone to the trouble of making a good stock it seems a shame not to get the end product right.

I don't think enough people make their own soups at home, perhaps because they think it's too much of a hassle, or possibly the ready-made 'fresh' soups on supermarket shelves prove too tempting. But there is something incredibly satisfying about a bowl of homemade soup, and it's a brilliant way of using up odds and ends of vegetables and other ingredients in the fridge and larder.

A soup can be as simple or as complicated as you like. Time and again I find that when too many ingredients have been added the essence of the soup gets a bit lost. For a simple puréed soup, I like to use just a little leek and onion as the base, but beyond this – and the main ingredient – little else is needed in the way of flavouring. The secret is not to cook the soup for too long, really just as much as it takes for the vegetables to become tender, then blend it. A good blender will give you a silky smooth soup and a better result than a food processor. Seasoning is also important – don't forget to taste for seasoning before you serve and re-season if necessary.

Naturally the soups on the menu vary with the seasons. Through the colder months I like to feature game, slow-cooked flavourful meat cuts, pulses and root veg, while in the height of summer cold soups really come into their own.

SUMMER VEGETABLE BROTH

This is a nice light broth using summer peas and beans. You can vary the vegetables according to what is available. Asparagus is a great addition when it's in season, and diced new potatoes will make the soup a bit more substantial.

Serves 4

1.5 litres vegetable stock

1 small leek, trimmed, cut into 1cm dice and washed

1 celery stick, peeled if necessary and cut into 5mm dice

salt and freshly ground black pepper

150g podded broad beans

100g podded peas

60g green or runner beans, cut into 5mm lengths

1 tbsp chopped parsley

1 tbsp chopped chives

Pour the vegetable stock into a large saucepan, add the leek and celery and bring to a simmer. Season lightly with salt and pepper and let simmer for 15 minutes.

Meanwhile, blanch the broad beans in boiling salted water for 3–4 minutes, then drain and refresh under the cold tap. Remove the tough skins from any larger broad beans; leave small ones as they are.

Add the peas and green beans to the simmering stock and cook for a further 10 minutes. Add the broad beans, chopped parsley and chives, and simmer for another 5 minutes. Re-season if necessary before serving.

CHILLED GOLDEN BEETROOT SOUP

This is a great soup to trick guests and keep them guessing as to what you are serving. Beetroot would be the last thing they would think of, but golden beet - one of several old varieties on the market - makes a stunning soup.

You can finish it with all sorts of things - horseradish will give the soup a kick, or you might prefer a little shredded ham or salted ox tongue.

Serves 4

400g medium yellow beetroot

salt and freshly ground black pepper

1 tbsp cold-pressed rapeseed or olive oil

1 small onion, peeled and roughly chopped

1 litre vegetable stock

To finish

cream, crème fraîche or soft goat's cheese

1 tbsp freshly grated horseradish

Cook the beetroot in a pan of salted water for about 1 hour until they feel tender when pierced with a knife. Drain and leave until cool enough to handle, then peel and roughly chop the beetroot.

Heat the oil in a large saucepan, add the onion, cover and cook gently for 3–4 minutes to soften. Add the vegetable stock, bring to the boil, season with a little salt and pepper and simmer for 30 minutes.

Add the beetroot, then remove from the heat. Purée in a blender until smooth, then pass the soup through a fine-meshed sieve into a large bowl. Re-season if necessary. Cool the soup down, then refrigerate for a few hours until well chilled or put it into the freezer if you're in a rush.

Serve in soup plates topped with a dollop of cream, crème fraîche or soft goat's cheese and a sprinkling of grated horseradish.

CHILLED GARDEN HERB SOUP

This soup has been appearing on my menus for years in various guises. You need to be careful with the herbs though, as more pungent varieties are likely to be too overpowering. Parsley, chervil and chives can be used in abundance, but herbs like lovage, coriander and tarragon should be added in moderation.

Finish the soup with goat's curd or a milder goat's cheese or crème fraîche, or serve it just as it is.

Serves 4–6

a good handful of parsley, washed
a good handful of chervil, washed
a good handful of basil, washed
1 tbsp cold-pressed rapeseed oil
1 small fennel bulb, roughly chopped
1 medium onion, peeled and roughly chopped
1 leek, trimmed, roughly chopped and washed
1 tbsp plain flour
1.5 litres vegetable stock
salt and freshly ground black pepper
about 10g chives
a few mint leaves

To finish (optional)
goat's curd, soft goat's cheese or crème fraîche
finely chopped herbs, such as chervil, chives and parsley

Break off the thicker stalks from the parsley, chervil and basil and set aside; keep the leaves separate.

Heat the rapeseed oil in a large saucepan and add the fennel, onion and leek. Cover and cook gently for 4–5 minutes until soft, stirring every so often. Add the flour and stir well, then gradually stir in the vegetable stock. Season to taste.

Bring to the boil, add the herb stalks and simmer gently for 20 minutes. Add the rest of the herbs, including the chives and mint leaves. Simmer for 2 minutes, no longer.

Purée the soup in a blender until smooth, then pass through a medium sieve (rather than a fine one, to let the herb bits through) into a bowl.

Set the bowl over another larger bowl of iced water to cool the soup down as quickly as possible (this helps to preserve its green colour). Re-season if necessary.

Serve the soup straight from the fridge. If you like, top with a dollop of goat's curd, goat's cheese or crème fraîche and a sprinkling of chopped herbs.

HORSERADISH SOUP

I first had this soup in Poland. It was so good that I vowed to make my own version and put it on the menu. We have loads of horseradish growing in the UK but don't seem to make much use of it, apart from the ubiquitous horseradish sauce for roast beef and the odd grating for a bloody Mary.

Serves 4

50g butter
1 onion, peeled and roughly chopped
1 large leek, trimmed, roughly chopped and washed
1 tbsp plain flour
1.5 litres hot vegetable stock
salt and freshly ground black pepper
100g freshly grated horseradish, or more to taste
1–2 tbsp double cream

Melt the butter in a large saucepan. Add the onion and leek, cover and cook gently without colouring for 3–4 minutes, stirring every so often, to soften. Stir in the flour and cook over a low heat for 30 seconds, then gradually stir in the vegetable stock. Bring to the boil, season and simmer for 30 minutes.

Add about two-thirds of the horseradish to the soup and simmer for 5 minutes, then take off the heat. Purée in a blender until smooth, then pass through a fine-meshed sieve into a clean saucepan.

Taste for seasoning and the horseradish, adding more to taste. You don't need to blend the soup again – the extra horseradish gives a nice texture. Add the cream, bring back to a simmer and serve.

SMOKED HADDOCK AND LEEK BROTH WITH POACHED QUAIL'S EGGS

Smoked haddock and leeks make a really great tasting soup. This is quite similar to a Cullen skink except that I've added some poached quail's eggs to it. I have a little trick of the trade here as you are probably wondering how the hell are you going to poach quail's eggs. You can use either Arbroath smokies (hot-smoked haddock) or natural smoked haddock.

Serves 4–6

2 leeks, trimmed
40g butter
½ tsp fennel seeds
1 tbsp plain flour
1 litre hot fish stock
200g natural smoked haddock
about 200ml milk
12 quail's eggs
about 100ml white wine vinegar
salt and freshly ground white pepper
1 tbsp chopped parsley
60ml double cream

Roughly chop one of the leeks, cut the other into rough 1cm dice and wash both thoroughly, keeping them separate.

Melt the butter in a large saucepan and add the chopped leek with the fennel seeds. Cook gently until softened, without colouring. Stir in the flour, then gradually add the hot fish stock, stirring well. Bring to the boil, lower the heat and simmer gently for 30 minutes.

Meanwhile, poach the smoked haddock in enough milk to cover in a small pan for 3–4 minutes. Drain over a bowl, reserving the milk. Add this poaching liquor to the soup along with a third of the haddock. Take off the heat.

Purée the soup in a blender until very smooth, then strain it through a fine-meshed sieve into a clean saucepan.

To poach the quail's eggs, bring a pan of water to the boil and have a bowl of cold water ready. Pour the wine vinegar into another bowl and carefully crack all the quail's eggs into it, using a small sharp knife to crack open the shells.

Now tip the quail's eggs and vinegar into the pan of simmering water. The eggs will separate and set. Poach for 1 minute, then carefully remove with a slotted spoon and place in the bowl of cold water.

Meanwhile, cook the diced leek in a little boiling salted water for 2–3 minutes until tender, then drain.

Flake the rest of the smoked haddock and add to the soup with the leek and chopped parsley. Bring to a simmer, stir in the cream and check the seasoning.

Place 2 or 3 poached quail's eggs in each warmed soup bowl and ladle the hot soup over them to serve.

COCKLE, PARSLEY AND CIDER BROTH

Cockles have a great flavour, better than their larger cousins clams, in my opinion, and a fraction of the price. That said, of course meatier clams can be used for this soup. You could even add a couple of handfuls of mussels if you like.

Cockles have a tendency to be a bit gritty, owing to the grooves in their shells, so make sure you wash them really thoroughly.

Serves 4

1kg live cockles
150ml cider
30g butter
1 onion, peeled and finely chopped
4 garlic cloves, peeled and crushed
25g plain flour
1 litre fish stock
2 tbsp finely chopped parsley
3–4 tbsp double cream
salt and freshly ground black pepper

To clean the cockles, leave them under slow running water for about 15 minutes, agitating them with your hands every so often to release any trapped sand. Give the cockles a final rinse and drain.

Put the cleaned cockles in a large saucepan with the cider. Cover with a tight-fitting lid and cook over a high heat for about 2–3 minutes, shaking the pan every so often, until the cockles open.

Drain the cockles in a colander over a bowl, to catch the cooking liquor, then strain the liquor through a fine-meshed sieve into another bowl and set aside.

Melt the butter in a clean saucepan and gently cook the onion and garlic for 3–4 minutes without colouring. Add the flour and stir over a low heat for 30 seconds, then gradually whisk in the strained cooking liquor and fish stock. Bring to the boil, lower the heat and simmer gently for 30 minutes. By now the liquid should have reduced by about one-third and have a good flavour.

In the meantime, remove about two-thirds of the cockles from their shells; leave the rest as they are.

Add the chopped parsley and cream to the soup and simmer for a couple of minutes. Taste and adjust the seasoning as necessary.

Divide all the cockles between warmed soup plates and pour the hot soup over them to serve.

JELLIED TOMATO SOUP WITH CRAYFISH AND WILD FENNEL

You may think this looks and sounds a bit fancy for me, but it is actually very straightforward. It's amazing how much flavour you can extract from a few really ripe tomatoes in the form of a clear jelly. You may need to order freshwater crayfish in advance from your fishmonger, or you could use lobster or crab.

Once you've made it, you can prepare yet another soup from the crayfish shells (see page 78). Also, the pulp left from making the jelly can be transformed into a tomato salsa for dipping or to use as a sauce for pasta: just cook the pulp in a pan over a low heat, season and spice up with a little chilli and coriander if you wish.

Serves 4–6

2 garlic cloves, peeled
1.5kg ripe tomatoes, halved
a few sprigs of basil
salt and freshly ground black pepper
300ml good-quality tomato juice
3–4 sheets of leaf gelatine (9–12g)
1 tbsp fennel seeds
1kg live freshwater crayfish
a few sprigs of wild fennel or dill

Add the garlic cloves to a pan of boiling water and blanch for 2 minutes, then drain and place in a food processor. Add the tomatoes, basil, some salt and pepper, and 250ml of the tomato juice. Process briefly to a coarse texture.

Line a colander with a double layer of muslin or a clean tea towel and set over a large bowl. Pour the tomato pulp into the colander, cover loosely and place in the fridge. Leave overnight to allow the juice to drip through slowly.

The next day you should have about 600–700ml of clear juice in the bowl. Gently squeeze the pulp to extract as much juice as possible.

Soak 3 sheets of gelatine (or 4 if you have more than 750ml tomato juice) in cold water to soften.

Meanwhile, take a small ladleful of the clear tomato juice and heat it in a pan. Squeeze the excess water from the gelatine leaves, then add them to the hot tomato juice and stir until dissolved; do not allow to boil. Add this to the rest of the strained juice with the remaining 50ml tomato juice and stir well. Cover and refrigerate for 1–2 hours until set.

In the meantime, bring a large saucepan of water to the boil with the fennel seeds and plenty of salt added. Plunge in the crayfish, bring back to the boil and simmer for 3 minutes, then drain in a colander and leave to cool a little. Carefully peel the crayfish tails; if the claws are large, crack them open to extract the meat.

To serve, break the jelly up a little, then spoon into serving bowls and top with the crayfish. Scatter over the fennel and serve.

CRAYFISH SOUP WITH CIDER BRANDY

The potential waste with crayfish, crabs, lobsters, and other crustaceans is pretty high if you don't put their shells to good use. All of a sudden, expensive shellfish like these become good value once you have used the shells to make a few bowls of rich velvety soup.

I've added a few splashes of Julian Temperley's Somerset cider brandy at the end here to give the soup a bit of a West Country kick.

Serves 6–8

the shells from a 1kg freshly cooked crayfish, any excess tail meat reserved
1 tbsp vegetable oil
1 small onion, peeled and roughly chopped
1 small leek, trimmed, roughly chopped and washed
2 celery sticks, roughly chopped
3 garlic cloves, peeled and roughly chopped
½ tsp fennel seeds
a pinch of saffron strands
a few sprigs of thyme
a couple of sprigs of tarragon
1 bay leaf
40g butter
3 tbsp plain flour
2 tbsp tomato purée
1 glass of white wine
1.5 litres fish stock
salt and freshly ground white pepper
100ml double cream
a few dashes of Somerset cider brandy

Chop up the crayfish shells. Heat the oil in a large heavy-based saucepan and add the crayfish shells with the vegetables. Fry over a high heat, stirring every so often, for about 5 minutes until they begin to colour. Add the garlic, fennel seeds, saffron, thyme, tarragon and bay leaf, and continue cooking for another 5 minutes or so.

Add the butter and once it has melted, stir in the flour. Cook over a medium heat for about 5 minutes, stirring frequently, until the mixture turns a dark sandy colour. Add the tomato purée, stir well and cook over a low heat for a minute or so. Add the wine, then slowly add the fish stock, stirring to avoid lumps. Bring to the boil, season with salt and pepper, and simmer for 1 hour.

Liquidise the soup, shells and all, in a strong blender or food processor until smooth, then strain through a fine-meshed sieve into a clean pan. You'll need to do this in batches.

Bring to a simmer, then add the cream and any crayfish tail meat. Re-season if necessary and stir in the cider brandy. Serve in warmed soup plates.

CHICKEN SOUP AND SEASONAL VARIATIONS

You can't beat a good bowl of creamy chicken soup at any time of the year. A raw carcass or two is the best option and your butcher may even give them to you, if you're lucky. You can get away with a carcass from a cooked bird but it won't give as full a flavour.

Through the year, have fun playing around with seasonal variations. Add wild mushrooms as they appear in the autumn and spring, and in the summer add peas and broad beans. Or put some crayfish or lobster shells into the soup and blend it up for a surf and turf option.

Serves 4–6

1 raw free-range chicken carcass, chopped

2 free-range chicken legs or just the thighs or drumsticks

1 onion, peeled and roughly chopped

1 leek, trimmed, roughly chopped and washed

10 black peppercorns

1 bay leaf

a few sprigs of thyme

a few sprigs of tarragon, leaves chopped, stalks reserved

1.5 litres chicken stock

60g butter, plus an extra couple of knobs

50g plain flour

salt and freshly ground white pepper

120g wild mushrooms (in season), cleaned and sliced if large

60ml double cream

Put the chicken carcass and legs into a pan with the onion, leek, peppercorns, bay leaf, thyme, tarragon stalks and chicken stock. Bring to the boil, lower the heat and simmer for 35–40 minutes.

Remove the chicken legs and set them aside on a plate. Strain the stock through a fine-meshed sieve into a jug. Melt the 60g butter in a clean pan over a medium heat and stir in the flour. Gradually add the strained stock, a ladleful at a time, stirring well to avoid lumps. Bring to the boil, season and simmer gently for 30 minutes.

Blend the soup with a hand-held blender, or use a free-standing blender to give it a nice silky finish.

Meanwhile, melt a couple of knobs of butter in a frying pan. Add the mushrooms and cook gently for 2–3 minutes without colouring them.

Remove the meat from the chicken and cut or tear it into even-sized pieces. Add to the soup with the mushrooms, cream and chopped tarragon leaves. Re-season if necessary and simmer for a minute or so before serving.

GROUSE AND AUTUMN VEGETABLE BROTH

A hearty broth is an excellent way to make good use of the carcass from a traditional roast grouse, or any game bird for that matter. Or if you've made the grouse salad (on page 65) you can enjoy this soup the following day. In addition to the autumnal early roots, you might like to add some seasonal wild mushrooms or a pulse, such as split green peas, pearl barley or lentils.

Serves 4–6

For the broth

the carcasses from 2 or more grouse (raw or roasted)

1 tbsp vegetable oil

1 small onion, peeled and roughly chopped

1 medium carrot, peeled and roughly chopped

2 garlic cloves, peeled and crushed

a couple of sprigs of thyme

4 juniper berries

a generous knob of butter

1 tbsp plain flour

1 tsp tomato purée

2 litres chicken stock

salt and freshly ground black pepper

To serve

1 small leek, trimmed

2 celery sticks, peeled to remove strings if necessary

1 medium carrot, peeled

a couple of green cabbage leaves

Chop each of the grouse carcasses into 4 or 5 pieces. Heat the oil in a large, heavy-based saucepan over a medium heat. Add the grouse carcasses with the onion, carrot, garlic, thyme and juniper berries and fry for 3–4 minutes, stirring every so often, until lightly coloured.

Add the butter and once it has melted, stir in the flour. Cook, stirring for a few minutes, then add the tomato purée and chicken stock. Bring to the boil, season with salt and pepper and simmer gently for an hour.

In the meantime, cut the leek, celery, carrot and cabbage roughly into 5mm pieces, washing the leek thoroughly after chopping.

Strain the broth through a fine-meshed sieve into a clean saucepan, reserving the pieces of carcass. Add the leek, celery and carrot and simmer for about 15 minutes or until they are tender. Add the cabbage and simmer for a further 5–6 minutes.

Meanwhile, remove as many bits of meat from the grouse carcasses as possible and add to the soup. Simmer for a final minute or two, re-season if necessary and serve in warmed soup plates.

MUTTON AND GREEN SPLIT PEA BROTH

Mutton is a great choice for a sustaining wintry broth enriched with pulses. I recommend using raw meat rather than leftovers, as you will get a much fuller flavoured broth. In my larder at home I always keep lots of different pulses as they are great for soups, salads and other dishes.

Serves 4–6

200g neck of mutton fillet

½ tsp chopped thyme leaves

1 onion, peeled and finely chopped

2 litres lamb or chicken stock

salt and freshly ground black pepper

1 medium carrot, peeled

1 medium parsnip, peeled

100–120g swede, peeled

1 small turnip, peeled

50g green split peas, soaked in cold water for 2–3 hours

1 tbsp chopped parsley

Cut the mutton roughly into 1cm dice and place in a large saucepan with the thyme and onion. Pour in the stock, season with salt and pepper and bring to the boil. Lower the heat and simmer for an hour until the mutton is more or less tender.

Meanwhile, cut the carrot, parsnip, swede and turnip into rough 1cm dice. Drain the split peas and add them to the soup with the vegetables. Simmer gently for another 30 minutes until the mutton, split peas and vegetables are tender.

Add the chopped parsley and simmer for a further 10 minutes. Check the seasoning and serve.

WILD RABBIT AND OYSTER MUSHROOM SOUP

Rabbits are cheap and plentiful and so are oyster mushrooms, in fact both ingredients are free if you happen to be a hunter-gatherer. If not, then a rabbit will cost you a few quid and you can save the saddle fillets for a salad or other dish.

Serves 4–6

1 wild rabbit
1 small leek, trimmed, roughly chopped and washed
1 small onion, peeled and roughly chopped
2 garlic cloves, peeled
a couple of sprigs of thyme
1 bay leaf
10 black peppercorns
2 litres chicken stock
salt and freshly ground black pepper
60g butter
50g plain flour
120g oyster mushrooms, cleaned
2–3 tbsp double cream
1 tbsp chopped parsley

Remove the fillets from the saddle of the rabbit (save them for another dish). Cut off the legs and half them at the joint, chopping through the bones.

Place the rabbit, leek, onion, garlic, herbs and peppercorns in a large saucepan. Pour in the chicken stock, season with salt and pepper and bring to the boil, then skim off any scum from the surface. Simmer for an hour, skimming every so often. If the leg meat is tender, remove and put to one side, otherwise leave in the pan.

Melt the butter in a small saucepan, stir in the flour and stir over a low heat for 20 seconds. Whisk this flour and butter paste into the simmering stock in small pieces. Continue to simmer gently, stirring occasionally for 20 minutes.

Strain the soup through a fine-meshed sieve into a clean pan. Cut the oyster mushrooms into even-sized chunks, add them to the soup and simmer for 10 minutes.

Meanwhile, strip the rabbit meat from the bones in bite-sized pieces and add to the soup with the cream and chopped parsley. Re-season if necessary before serving in warmed soup plates or bowls.

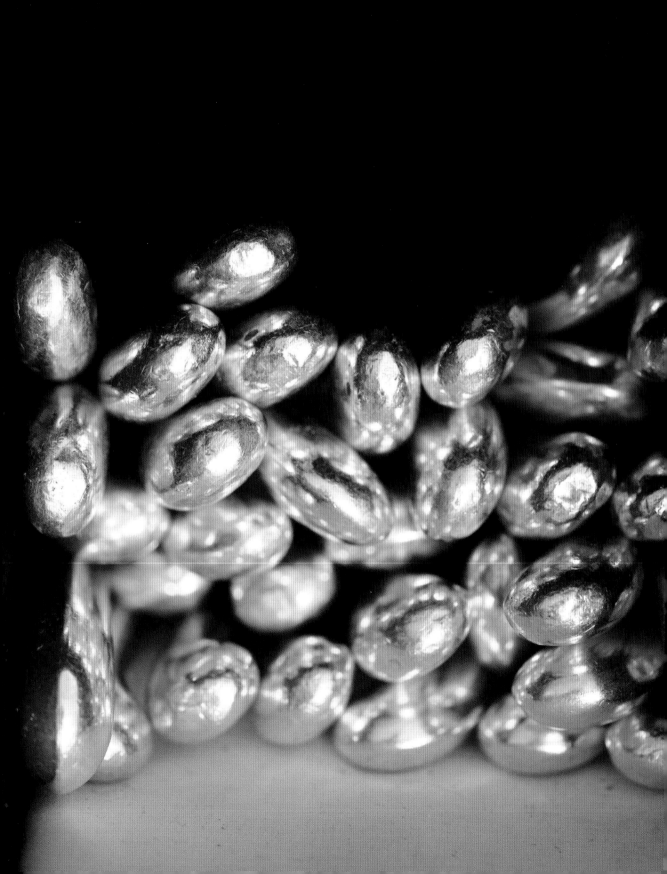

ON TOAST

A few years back when we opened the Rivington Grill in Shoreditch I developed an 'on toast' section for the menu. It gave customers the option to indulge in a snack without feeling they had to be part of the whole dining experience. Taking some of the formality out of restaurant dining has always appealed to me. In my view, restaurants are somewhere to socialise and eat rather than be reserved just for special occasions.

At the Oyster & Chop House, we don't have an 'on toast' section as such, but I often serve these dishes as starters and bar snacks. Putting ingredients on toast is an ideal way to show off a great seasonal ingredient, such as asparagus, broad beans, heritage tomatoes or wild mushrooms. It is also an opportunity to revisit classics, such as Welsh rabbit and pilchards on toast. I love playing around with these old-fashioned recipes and coming up with interesting variations, such as Smoked haddock rabbit and Mackerel and tomatoes on toast.

It goes without saying that good-quality bread is essential – a bloomer-type loaf is ideal, cut into slices about 1cm thick. There's really no limit to the things you can put on toast. Use the ideas in this chapter as a platform for developing your own toast creations.

ASPARAGUS ON TOAST WITH DORSET DRUM CHEDDAR

During its relatively short season I like to serve home-grown asparagus in as many different ways as possible. Serving it on toast turns it into a sophisticated snack. I've topped this with one of my favourite cheeses, Dorset drum Cheddar, which comes from Denhay Farm, just outside Bridport in West Dorset.

Serves 4

300–350g medium asparagus spears
salt and freshly ground black pepper
a couple of generous knobs of butter
4 slices of brown or white, bloomer-type bread
100g piece of mature Dorset drum Cheddar cheese
3–4 tbsp cold-pressed rapeseed oil

To cook the asparagus, bring a pan of well-salted water to the boil. Cut off and discard the woody ends of the asparagus, then add to the pan. Simmer for 4–5 minutes or until just tender. Drain and trim the base of the spears so they are roughly the same length as the bread slices.

Put the asparagus trimmings into a blender and process briefly to a rough purée. Reheat in a pan with the butter and season to taste.

Toast the bread on both sides. Spread generously with the asparagus purée and lay the hot or warm asparagus on top. Using a peeler or sharp knife, shave the cheese over the top and drizzle with the rapeseed oil.

RED MULLET ON TOAST WITH CRUSHED BROAD BEANS AND PEAS

This is a popular dish at the Oyster & Fish House in Lyme Regis. It really says summer when it arrives at the table, especially when you have a great sea view. You could use red gurnard or even mackerel fillets instead of red mullet.

Serves 4

250g podded young broad beans
salt and freshly ground black pepper
a couple of generous knobs of butter
60g podded peas
4 small red mullet fillets, about 80g, or 2 halved fillets from a larger fish
4 slices of brown or white, bloomer-type bread
½ tbsp cider vinegar
1½ tbsp cold-pressed rapeseed oil
a handful of pea shoots (if available)

Cook the broad beans in boiling salted water for 3–4 minutes (or a little longer if they are large) until tender. Drain them and blend to a coarse purée in a food processor, adding a little butter and seasoning to taste; keep warm.

Cook the peas in boiling salted water for a couple of minutes until tender. Drain and set aside.

Melt the rest of the butter in a heavy or non-stick frying pan. Season the red mullet fillets and fry them, skin side down first, over a medium heat for a couple of minutes on each side.

Toast the bread on both sides. Meanwhile, whisk the cider vinegar and rapeseed oil together to make a dressing and season with salt and pepper.

Spread the broad bean purée generously on the toasts and top with the red mullet. Arrange the peas and pea shoots, if using, around the toasts and spoon the dressing over them to serve.

SMOKED HADDOCK RABBIT

This fishy variation on a classic Welsh rabbit makes an excellent brunch dish or teatime snack. You can use either Arbroath smokies or natural smoked haddock.

Serves 4

150–200g natural smoked haddock
about 160ml milk for poaching
5 tbsp stout
5 tbsp double cream
75g Caerphilly cheese, grated
75g Cheddar cheese, grated
2 free-range egg yolks
2 tsp Worcestershire sauce, or more to taste
1 tsp English mustard
salt and freshly ground black pepper
4 slices of brown or white, bloomer-type bread

Poach the smoked haddock in gently simmering milk to cover for 3–4 minutes, then drain. Leave to cool a little, then remove the skin and any bones and flake the haddock flesh.

In a small heavy-based pan, simmer the stout until it has reduced by half. Add the cream and again reduce this by half until it is really thick. Leave to cool a little, then mix in the grated cheese, followed by the egg yolks, Worcestershire sauce and mustard. Stir in the flaked haddock and season with salt and pepper to taste.

Preheat the grill to medium. Toast the bread on both sides. Spread the cheese mixture thickly on top of the toasts, about 1cm thick and right to the edges to avoid them burning under the grill. Place under the grill until the topping is nicely browned, then serve.

MACKEREL AND TOMATOES ON TOAST

A great snack or summery starter. Use a selection of home-grown tomato varieties and cook the mackerel as for my Fish house salad (on page 64).

Serves 4

about 200g mixed tomatoes
4 cooked medium or 8 small mackerel fillets
sea salt and freshly ground black pepper
4 slices of brown or white, bloomer-type bread
a few small herb or salad leaves (optional)

Turn the oven to its lowest setting (with the fan on). Halve small tomatoes; cut large ones into wedges. Lay on a baking tray and dry in the oven for 6–7 hours or overnight until they've lost about a third of their weight. Ovens vary so check after a few hours.

Break the mackerel into pieces and gently mix with some of their oily cooking liquor and the tomatoes. Season to taste. Toast the bread on both sides. Top with the mackerel and tomato mixture and scatter over the herb or salad leaves, if using.

SMOKED COD'S ROE WITH HORSERADISH BUTTER

I love cod's roe, but you rarely see it on fishmongers' slabs or menus these days. The sustainability issue may have taken it off the culinary map, but I see no reason to disregard the roe of a sustainably caught fish.

Serves 4

150–200g smoked cod's roe
1 tbsp freshly grated horseradish
50–60g softened butter
4 slices of brown or white, bloomer-type bread

Thinly slice the cod's roe (unless it's soft enough to spread). Mix the horseradish with the butter. Toast the bread on both sides, spread generously with the horseradish butter and top with the cod's roe.

DORSET CRAB ON TOAST

This is on a par with a good crab sandwich. If possible, buy a live crab and cook and prepare it yourself (using the shells for a soup), or get your fishmonger to do it for you. I'm always a bit suspicious of pre-packed crab meat unless you have a very trustworthy source. The brown crab meat can be a little wet once prepared; if so, drain off the watery juices and mix in some fresh white or brown breadcrumbs to thicken it up a bit.

Serves 4

300–350g brown crab meat
150–200g white crab meat
salt and freshly ground white pepper
2–3 tbsp good-quality mayonnaise
4 slices of good-quality brown bread
butter for spreading
1 small lemon, quartered, to serve

Break up the brown crab meat in a bowl using a fork, season with salt and pepper and mix with mayonnaise to taste.

Toast the bread on both sides and spread with butter. Spoon the brown crab onto the toast and scatter over the white meat. Grind over some pepper and serve with lemon wedges.

WOOD PIGEON ON TOAST WITH WILD MUSHROOMS

You can use just about any game bird in season for this simple starter or snack, including grouse, widgeon and partridge. Buy or gather whatever mushrooms are in season – either as a mix or as a singular variety.

Serves 4

2 oven-ready pigeons, preferably with their livers (otherwise, buy 120g chicken or duck livers)

a few generous knobs of butter

2 shallots, peeled and finely chopped

1 garlic clove, peeled and crushed

salt and freshly ground black pepper

2 tbsp sherry

150–200g wild mushrooms, cleaned

1 tbsp sherry vinegar

3 tbsp walnut oil

4 slices of brown or white, bloomer-type bread

a handful of small salad leaves, washed and dried

Preheat the oven to 220°C/gas mark 7. Clean the pigeon livers, cut into even-sized pieces and pat dry with kitchen paper. Heat a good knob of butter in a frying pan and fry the shallots and garlic for a minute.

Season the livers with salt and pepper, add to the pan and fry, stirring, over a medium heat for 2–3 minutes. Stir in the sherry, then take off the heat.

Rub the pigeon breasts with butter, season and place the birds in a small roasting tin. Roast in the oven for 10–15 minutes, keeping the meat nice and pink.

Meanwhile, chop the liver mixture as coarsely or finely as you wish. Re-season if necessary. Sauté the mushrooms in a little butter for a few minutes and season to taste.

For the dressing, whisk the sherry vinegar with the walnut oil and some salt and pepper.

Toast the bread on both sides. Remove the breasts from the pigeon and cut into 4 or 5 slices. Spread the toasts with the liver and top with the pigeon breast slices. Shred any leg meat from the birds, toss with the salad leaves and dressing, and arrange around the toasts. Scatter the mushrooms on top.

CHOPPED LIVERS ON TOAST

This is such a simple, inexpensive dish to knock up quickly at home. You can use either chicken or duck livers, preferably fresh rather than frozen though the latter will do.

Serves 4

250g fresh chicken or duck livers, cleaned

100g butter

2 large shallots, peeled and finely chopped

1 garlic clove, peeled and crushed

salt and freshly ground black pepper

4 slices of brown or white, bloomer-type bread

a handful of land cress, young watercress or other small salad leaves, washed and dried

Cut the livers into small, even-sized chunks. Melt half the butter in a saucepan and gently cook the shallots and garlic for 3–4 minutes, stirring every so often, until soft. Take off the heat.

Pat the chicken livers dry with kitchen paper and season with salt and pepper. Melt the rest of the butter in a frying pan until it begins to foam. Add the livers and cook them for a couple of minutes on each side. Transfer to a board and chop finely, or give the livers just a few seconds in a food processor.

Toast the bread on both sides. Mix the livers with the shallots and garlic. Re-season if necessary and spoon generously on to the toasts. Top with the cress and serve.

FISH

The fish section at the Oyster & Chop House is relatively small as the main emphasis is on meat, but I always like to have an interesting selection of fish dishes on the menu. I prefer to offer customers fish that they would not usually find in shops or on the fishmonger's slab.

Many of our seafish species are overlooked, but to keep stocks at a respectable level, we need to be eating a wide variety of fish – not just the ones we know best. The other great thing with lesser-known species is that I can put them on the menu at a reasonable price. If I only offered deep-fried cod and haddock it would make our fish and chips look a tad expensive, especially if customers compare prices to those of high street fish 'n' chip shops, which generally sell cheaper frozen fish. I wouldn't think twice about offering less fashionable grey mullet, ling or coley on the menu, alongside highly prized John Dory or turbot.

Keeping tabs on what is (and what's not) on the endangered list is tricky these days, as it changes constantly and even fishmongers are not always up to speed on current fishy affairs. At home you can keep informed by logging onto www.fishonline.org – The Marine Conservation Society's website that provides up-to-date information on currently sustainable species.

I'm inclined to think that restaurant menus and informative food writing is really the way to get people eating second and third division fish. Think twice and question your fishmonger the next time you buy fish to cook at home.

ROASTED SHELLFISH PLATTER

A platter of mixed shellfish is a great indulgent dish to order in a restaurant or serve for a dinner party. You can really use any kind of shellfish but try to limit the selection to about 4 varieties, or you will have too many different cooking times to contend with.

I like to serve the shellfish scattered with some seashore vegetables, to add that extra little taste of the sea. You can also use wild garlic leaves or hedgerow garlic instead of garlic cloves.

Serves 2–4

1 live lobster, about 700g

2–3 tbsp cold-pressed rapeseed oil

salt and freshly ground black pepper

4 medium or 12 queen scallops, cleaned, in the half-shell

500g cockles, clams or mussels (or a combination), cleaned

6 razor clams

120g butter

6 garlic cloves, peeled and crushed

a couple of handfuls of seashore vegetable(s), such as sea beet, samphire or sea purslane

2 tbsp chopped parsley

Place the lobster in the freezer an hour or so before cooking to make them sleepy (deemed to be the most humane way of preparing live lobsters for cooking). Preheat the oven to 220°C/gas mark 7.

Heat a large roasting tray in the oven for about 10 minutes, adding the rapeseed oil for the last couple of minutes. Split the lobster in half through the head and down the back, using a heavy, sharp knife, and crack open the claws. Season the lobster and lay flesh-side down in the roasting tray. Roast in the oven for about 10 minutes.

Season the scallops and cockles (or ordinary clams or mussels). Add to the roasting tray and return to the oven for a further 5 minutes.

Finally add the razor clams, butter and garlic and roast in the oven for a further few minutes until they are just opened.

Meanwhile, plunge the seashore vegetable(s) into a pan of boiling lightly salted water and blanch for 1 minute, then drain thoroughly.

Remove the roasting tray from the oven and toss in the seashore vegetable(s) and chopped parsley. Transfer to a warmed serving dish and serve at once.

ROASTED 'WILDERNESS CRAYFISH' FLAMED WITH CIDER BRANDY

After a non-productive day of salmon fishing in Scotland last year, I came across an article on crayfish in a fishing magazine, written by a friend of mine, Neil Patterson. Apparently, red signal crayfish, which have become so prolific in our waters, were causing havoc for trout fishing on his stretch of the River Kennet 'the Wilderness'. I decided to help out by putting some of his signal crayfish on the menu. Every week the river keepers drop off crayfish for us and I feed them at the bar for their travels and to thank them for doing their bit for conservation.

Serves 4

2kg live freshwater crayfish
sea salt and freshly ground black pepper
100g butter
150ml Somerset cider brandy

Preheat the oven to 220°C/gas mark 7 and heat a roasting tray, large enough to take all of the crayfish, in the oven. Add the crayfish, season with salt and pepper and roast for 10 minutes.

Take the tray out of the oven and place it on the hob over a medium heat. Add the butter and stir to coat the crayfish, then stand back a little and carefully add the cider brandy. It will ignite (well hopefully, otherwise you could use a long match). If you have a tabletop gas stove you can do this at the table.

As soon as the flames have died down, serve the crayfish, providing everyone with finger bowls and extra napkins.

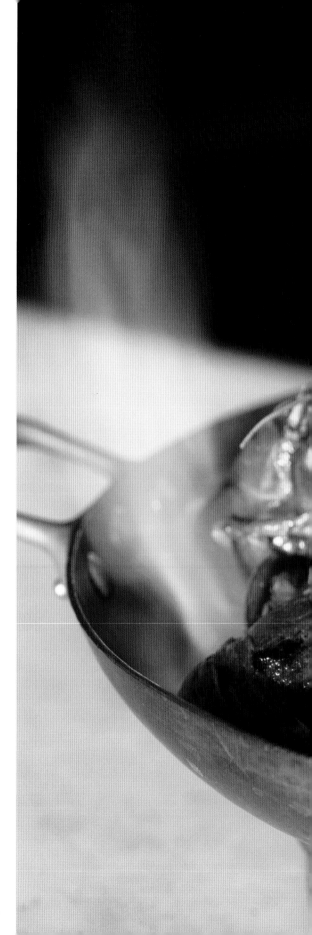

SCALLOPS WITH RAMSONS AND WILD BOAR BACON

Commonly called wild garlic, wide-leaved aromatic ramsons are gathered from woodlands during early spring before they flower. On the menu, they are called ramsons to distinguish them from hedgerow garlic and three-cornered garlic, which also go under the generic term 'wild garlic'. Peter Gott of Sillfield Farm in Cumbria supplies our wild boar streaky bacon, which is top-notch stuff.

Serves 4

16–20 medium hand-dived scallops, cleaned and left in the half-shell
8–12 rashers of streaky wild boar bacon
150g butter
salt and freshly ground black pepper
a couple of handfuls of ramsons

Remove the scallops from their half-shells and set aside. Warm the shells in a very low oven or somewhere similarly warm.

Cut the bacon into rough 5mm dice and cook gently in a dry frying pan for 3–4 minutes until lightly coloured. Remove the bacon from the pan with a slotted spoon, keeping the fat in the pan.

In a clean heavy-based frying pan, heat half of the butter. Season the scallops, add to the pan and fry over a high heat for a minute on each side until nicely coloured.

At the same time, melt the rest of the butter in the pan with the bacon fat and heat until almost foaming. Add the ramsons and cook for about 20 seconds until wilted, turning them with a spoon so they don't colour. Divide the ramsons between the scallop shells.

Lay the scallops on top of the ramsons. Toss the bacon into the butter remaining in the scallop pan, warm quickly, then spoon over the scallops and serve straight away.

GRIDDLED SQUID WITH BROAD BEAN RELISH

Squid lends itself to various cooking techniques apart from deep-frying, though I love it cooked that way. Spicing it up a little before cooking in a griddle pan and serving with a fresh-tasting relish is a great option.

Serves 4

500–600g cleaned squid, including tentacles
a little vegetable oil for brushing

For the broad bean relish
3–4 tbsp cold-pressed rapeseed oil
1 small onion, peeled and finely chopped
1 garlic clove, peeled and crushed
1 tsp cumin seeds
1 medium red chilli, deseeded and finely chopped
6 firm tomatoes, skinned and finely chopped
salt and freshly ground black pepper
80–100g podded broad beans
1 tbsp chopped coriander leaves

First make the broad bean relish. Heat the rapeseed oil in a saucepan and gently cook the onion and garlic with the cumin and chilli for 3–4 minutes, stirring every so often, until soft. Add the tomatoes, season with salt and pepper and simmer gently for about 10–12 minutes until they have softened.

Meanwhile, cook the broad beans in boiling salted water for 2–3 minutes, then drain and run under the cold tap briefly. Remove the skins from any large beans if you wish before adding them all to the tomato sauce. Continue simmering for about 5 minutes, adding a little water if the mixture seems dry. Re-season if necessary, add the chopped coriander and take off the heat.

Heat up a ridged griddle or heavy-based frying pan over a high heat. Cut the squid pouches into rough 4–5cm squares, season and brush with oil. Add to the hot griddle or pan with the tentacles and cook for 1–2 minutes on each side.

Arrange the squid on warmed plates and spoon over the broad bean relish to serve.

RED MULLET WITH ROSEMARY

In France red mullet is sometimes called *bécasse de mer*, meaning 'woodcock of the sea' as, like the game bird, the livers are highly prized. Red mullet are generally sold with their guts intact as the less their delicate flesh is handled the better.

Serves 4

4 very fresh red mullet, about 250–300g each, descaled and gutted, livers reserved

salt and freshly ground black pepper

1 tbsp cold-pressed rapeseed oil

25g unsalted butter

2 small garlic cloves (unpeeled)

a few sprigs of rosemary leaves, chopped

Set aside the fish livers. Season the fish with salt and pepper. Heat the rapeseed oil and butter in a non-stick frying pan over a medium-low heat, add the whole fish with the garlic cloves and cook for about 5–6 minutes on each side. Remove the fish from the pan to a warmed plate and keep warm.

Remove the garlic from the pan and peel and chop the cloves. Mix with the livers and rosemary.

Return the pan to the heat, add the liver mixture and fry for just 30 seconds, then mash a little with a fork. Spoon over the red mullet and serve.

COLEY WITH SEA SPINACH AND BROWN SHRIMPS

I've started using coley lately as I'm a bit concerned that pollack may be becoming overfished. I may be wrong but last summer in Lyme Bay, Dorset, pollack were pretty scarce.

If you live on the coast you'll have access to sea spinach or sea beet, which grows wild along beaches and paths and is easily recognisable. It has such a great flavour and it's free. Otherwise you could use ordinary spinach.

Serves 4

4 thick fillets of coley, about 180–200g each, skinned

sea salt and freshly ground black pepper

1 tbsp cold-pressed rapeseed oil

120g butter

a couple of handfuls of sea spinach (about 400g), washed and trimmed of any thick stalks

80g peeled brown shrimps

juice of ¼ lemon

Check the fish for any small bones, then lay the fillets on a tray and scatter generously with sea salt. Leave for 30 minutes, then rinse under cold water and dry on kitchen paper. Season with pepper.

Heat the rapeseed oil in a frying pan and add 50g of the butter. When foaming, add the coley fillets, skinned side up, and cook over a medium heat for 3–4 minutes on each side until golden.

Meanwhile, bring a pan of lightly salted water to the boil. Add the sea spinach and cook for 1 minute, then drain well. Melt half of the remaining butter in a pan, add the sea spinach, toss well and season with salt and pepper to taste.

Quickly heat the rest of the butter in a frying pan until foaming, add the shrimps with the lemon juice and briefly warm through.

Scatter the sea spinach onto warmed plates, place the coley fillets on top and spoon the shrimps over the coley to serve.

SPICY GLAZED HUSS WITH CRISPY SHALLOTS

Huss, or dogfish as it is also called, is an underestimated fish. For years it has been an item in fish 'n' chip shops where it is sold as 'rock salmon' or 'rock', as a cheaper alternative to fried cod or haddock. The glaze in this recipe works well and gives the humble fish a rather different image.

Serves 4

1–1.2kg huss, skinned

For the marinade
2 tbsp rapeseed oil
3 medium shallots, peeled and roughly chopped
4 garlic cloves, peeled and crushed
30–40g fresh root ginger, scraped and finely grated
1 small red chilli, with seeds, roughly chopped
1 tsp fennel seeds
1 tsp cumin seeds
2 tsp tomato purée
1 tbsp clear honey
1½ tsp dark brown molasses sugar or brown sugar
1½ tsp Worcestershire sauce
1 tbsp HP sauce
1 tbsp tomato ketchup
juice of 2 limes
sea salt and freshly ground black pepper

For the crispy shallots
vegetable oil for deep-frying
2 tbsp self-raising flour
100–120ml milk
4 large shallots, peeled, halved and thinly sliced

To prepare the marinade, heat the rapeseed oil in a heavy-based saucepan and gently cook the shallots, garlic, ginger, chilli and fennel and cumin seeds for 2–3 minutes. Add the rest of the ingredients, stir in 100ml water and season lightly. Bring to the boil, reduce the heat and simmer for 3–4 minutes. Let cool slightly, then process the marinade in a blender until smooth. Transfer to a bowl and leave to cool.

Split the huss lengthways down the middle through the bone, then cut into 10–12cm lengths. Place the fish pieces in a shallow dish, pour the marinade over them and turn to coat. Cover the dish with cling film and leave to marinate in the fridge for 2–3 hours.

Preheat the oven to 200°C/gas mark 6. Remove the huss from the dish and lay on a roasting tray, reserving the marinade. Spoon a couple of tablespoonfuls of the marinade over the fish and place in the oven. Bake for 15–20 minutes until just cooked through, basting with extra marinade a few times during cooking.

Meanwhile, for the crispy shallots, heat an 8cm depth of oil in a deep-fat fryer or other suitable deep, heavy pan to 160–180°C. Have 2 bowls ready, one with the flour and the other with the milk. Season the flour with salt and pepper.

Coat the shallots in the seasoned flour, shaking off any excess, then pass them through the milk and again through the flour, shaking off excess. Deep-fry the shallots in 2 or 3 batches, for 2–3 minutes until golden, turning them every so often to ensure they colour evenly. Remove with a slotted spoon and drain on kitchen paper.

Place a huss fillet on each warmed plate and top with the crispy shallots to serve.

LING WITH CREAMED PEAS, LEEKS AND BACON

Ling is not commonplace on fish counters, but it is a truly great choice. Firm-fleshed and full of flavour, it really takes to any kind of cooking – from grilling to deep-frying. I think you will be pleasantly surprised by the taste and texture of this third division fish.

Serves 4

4 thick fillets of ling, about 200g each, with skin

salt and freshly ground black pepper

150g freshly podded peas (about 300g before podding), or frozen peas

100g butter

6 rashers of streaky bacon, derinded and finely chopped

1 medium or 2 small leeks, trimmed, cut into rough 1cm squares and washed

200ml double cream

2 tbsp vegetable oil

Season the ling fillets with salt and pepper. Add the peas to a pan of salted water and simmer for 4–5 minutes or until tender, then drain.

In the meantime, melt half of the butter in a heavy-based saucepan and add the bacon and leek. Cover and cook gently over a medium-low heat for 3–4 minutes, stirring every so often, until the leek is soft.

Roughly chop the peas and add them to the leek and bacon with the cream. Season with salt and pepper and simmer for a few minutes until the cream has reduced and is just coating the peas.

Meanwhile, heat the oil in a non-stick frying pan over a medium-high heat and add the ling fillets, skin side down. Cook for 3–4 minutes until nicely coloured, then turn the fillets and add the rest of the butter to the pan. Fry for a couple of minutes until the fish is just cooked through.

To serve, spoon the creamed peas, leeks and bacon onto warmed plates and place the fish on top.

THORNBACK RAY WITH FRIED EGG, CAPERS AND ANCHOVIES

On a whim I thought I'd like to try cooking a fishy version of the classic veal Holstein. Thornback ray seemed an obvious choice as, once filleted, it has an unusual meaty texture. The dish started life at the Oyster & Fish House in Lyme Regis but we often serve it in London.

Serves 4

4 fillets from a medium ray wing, about 170g each

salt and freshly ground black pepper

2–3 tbsp plain flour

1 free-range large egg, beaten

50–60g fresh white breadcrumbs

2–3 tbsp vegetable oil

100g butter

4 free-range medium eggs

2 tbsp large capers

1 tbsp chopped parsley

8 anchovy fillets, halved lengthways

Warm the oven to its lowest setting. Season the ray fillets with salt and pepper. Have 3 dishes ready, one with the flour, one with the beaten egg and the third with the breadcrumbs. One at a time, coat the fish fillets in the flour, shaking off any excess, then pass through the egg and finally coat in the breadcrumbs.

You will probably need to cook the fish in a couple of batches. Heat the oil in a large frying pan and fry the ray fillets for 2–3 minutes on each side, adding a knob of butter once you've turned them over. Keep warm in a low oven.

Melt a little more butter in a non-stick frying pan and gently fry the eggs for a couple of minutes until the white has just set.

Heat the remaining butter in a pan until foaming, add the capers and chopped parsley and take off the heat. Lay a ray fillet on each warmed plate, place a fried egg on top and arrange the anchovy strips around the egg white. Spoon the butter and capers over the egg and serve.

MONKFISH CHEEK AND FENNEL PIE

Monkfish, cod and skate cheeks are a bit easier to get hold of these days, with the increased demand from restaurants. A few years ago you may have got a slightly odd look from your fishmonger if you had asked for them.

Serves 4

about 1 litre fish stock

2 fennel bulbs, trimmed

450–500g monkfish cheeks, trimmed and halved if large

70g butter

60g plain flour

sea salt and freshly ground black pepper

2 tbsp chopped parsley

2 tbsp double cream

For the topping

1–1.2kg potatoes (for mashing), peeled and quartered

50–60g butter

a little milk

2–3 tbsp fresh white breadcrumbs

Bring the fish stock to the boil in a saucepan. Meanwhile, quarter the fennel bulb, cut into 2cm chunks and separate the layers. Add the fennel to the stock and simmer for 6–7 minutes until tender, then remove with a slotted spoon and leave to cool on a plate.

Add the monkfish cheeks to the stock and simmer for 2–3 minutes, then drain in a colander over a bowl to reserve the stock.

Melt the butter in a heavy-based saucepan, stir in the flour and cook, stirring, over a low heat for about 30 seconds. Gradually whisk in the hot stock, keeping the sauce smooth. Season, then simmer gently for about 30–40 minutes. The sauce should be really quite thick by now; if not, let it simmer for a little longer.

Meanwhile, for the topping, cook the potatoes in a pan of salted water until tender. Drain well and return to the pan over a low heat to dry out for 30 seconds or so. Take off the heat and mash thoroughly, incorporating the butter and a little milk. Season with salt and pepper to taste.

Preheat the oven to 200°C/gas mark 6. Stir the monkfish cheeks, fennel, chopped parsley and cream into the sauce. Re-season if necessary, then transfer to a large pie dish or individual ones.

Spoon or pipe the mashed potato onto the pies and scatter over the breadcrumbs. Bake for 30 minutes (or 20 minutes for individual pies) until the topping is golden brown and the filling is hot.

MEAT

We cook almost all of our meat on the bone. Not only is the flavour generally much better, the portions look more generous and the meat shrinks less during cooking. At the Oyster & Chop House, we present customers with a selection of the raw meat cuts on a long wooden board, so they can have a look at them before they choose what to order. This invariably raises a few eyebrows and gets the taste buds tingling. In fact, it's now become something of a feature at the restaurant.

Here I've tried to cover the complete range of cuts we use for grilling and slow-cooking – all of them on the bone except the hanger steak. This is a cut I'd recommend you try. It does call for more chewing than familiar steaks like sirloin or fillet, but it has the most memorable flavour. Even as I was writing, I was still thinking up new possibilities for cuts on the bone together with my butchers – the rib edge steak was a last-minute addition.

Cooking meat on the bone at home has the same rewards as it does in the restaurant. The idea of this fully illustrated guide is to enable you to see exactly how the cuts should look – perhaps even take the book along when you go shopping. It's often difficult to explain to your butcher exactly what it is you're after if it's not displayed on the counter and it can be a bit awkward, especially if there's a lengthy queue. So here you go, just hand the book over, point at the cut you're after and ask for as many as you need. Hopefully you'll have an obliging butcher …

BEEF

There is always a lot of confusion about buying beef. How long should it be hung for? What breed should I buy? Hanging won't necessarily tenderise meat. If the animal is relaxed when it is slaughtered then you will generally have more tender meat, but not if it is stressed. The norm for beef is 28 days hanging. Some butchers go beyond this, but their carcasses will need a lot more trimming of oxidised meat.

Various different breeds appear on our menus, from tiny miniature Dexters to Galloways, Devon Ruby Reds, White Park and Aberdeen Angus. The breed doesn't necessarily determine the eating quality, although many cattle are cross-bred specifically for the table, which can determine factors such as fat marbling in the meat, fat cover and the size of the beast.

Cuts for grilling

FILLET ON-THE-BONE 250–350G

Fillet steak is a popular item on many restaurant menus, yet more often than not, it is the most disappointing cut, both in terms of flavour and value for money.

Typically, fillets are stripped off the carcass soon after the animal is slaughtered, to avoid weight loss during hanging as they have such a high market price tag. The fillets are then generally vacuum packed for storage and never have the opportunity to gain any flavour from maturing.

One of our butchers, Peter Allen, introduced me to fillet on-the-bone a few years back and it's been on the Oyster & Chop House menu day in, day out, ever since we opened.

The main advantage of fillet on-the-bone is the flavour. As it stays on the carcass with the sirloin during hanging, the flavour has time to mature. And, because it is attached to the bone, the cut has a more generous look about it. We leave the flavourful outer bark on the meat too. Most restaurants would fully trim it, so there is little left except the pure eye of meat, but I don't like the customer to miss out.

SIRLOIN ON-THE-BONE 300–350G

Rather like fillet on-the-bone, this prime steak has a good presence on the plate and an excellent flavour. The fat covering further enhances the taste, but you may prefer to remove a little of it before cooking for a leaner appearance.

PORTERHOUSE 800G–1KG FOR 2 OR 3

In Italy this is the Tuscan signature dish known as *Bistecca alla Fiorentina*, which traditionally uses the Chianna breed of cattle. It should be cut from the rear end of the short loin, so that the centre-cut fillet sits on the bone alongside the sirloin. This is a classic dish for two or three people to share. The origin of the name is unclear, but suggests a link to the old public ale houses, which served the dark ale 'porter' and were frequented by market porters. As we are so close to Smithfield, it sits on the menu very comfortably, though the term Porterhouse is more common in American steak houses than here.

When cooking, I would suggest a little less heat on the fillet side as it will cook much more quickly than the sirloin. If possible, position the fillet at the edge of your grill or hang it over one side of the griddle pan once it's been sealed all over, then you should end up with both sides cooked evenly.

WING RIB 300–350G

Also known as club steak, this has a fairly loose definition and is generally cut from the wing rib, which lies between the rib and the sirloin, although sometimes it is cut from the sirloin as the yield of steaks from the wing rib is rather limited. The advantage of this steak for me, is that you do tend to get more of the flavour of the rib together with the higher inner muscle fat content, which lends a sweeter flavour once cooked.

FILLET ON-THE-BONE

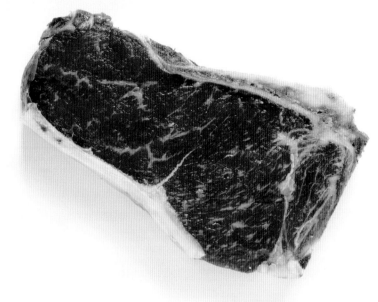

SIRLOIN ON-THE-BONE

PORTERHOUSE

WING RIB

RIB STEAK 300-350G OR 800-1KG FOR 2

This is the classic *cote de boeuf*, which you will often see on French restaurant menus. It can be cut either for one or two people, although cutting a single serving steak can be a problem with a larger beast because of the size of the bone. A straightforward cut between the bones will be too large for one serving, so you'll need to persuade your butcher to cut down the centre of the bone with his band saw to give you a good sized single portion.

The beauty of a rib steak is the heavier marbling and inner fat, which melts during cooking to give that unique sweetness to the meat.

RUMP ON-THE-BONE 600-800G FOR 2 OR 3

Rump steak can be a tricky cut as it comprises several muscles, which have varying degrees of tenderness. If you're not looking to do too much chewing, then you might be disappointed with this cut, but if you like a steak with texture and character, you'll appreciate the excellent flavour.

You could persuade your butcher to remove the outer muscles and just cut through the bone including the inner muscle, but for me a cut like rump on-the-bone for two or three people makes interesting eating, rather like the Porterhouse.

HANGER STEAK 180-220G

This is one of my favourite steaks but it's no longer common in the UK and unfortunately seems to be a forgotten cut. In the past, butchers certainly knew how good it was, as they would often keep it for themselves to take home as a perk, hence it's original name 'butcher's steak'. In France it is known as *onglet* and is a popular cut in brasseries. I've adopted the American term hanger in the restaurant as it prompts the customer to ask what it is.

Hanger is not the most tender of steaks, but it's the most flavoursome cut on the beast. In fact, it takes on some of the flavour of the kidney, which it is situated just below in the diaphragm.

The complete hanger, cut straight from the carcass, has a connective sinew running along the centre, which you can cut either side of. Occasionally it's possible to get a couple of good-sized steaks from each piece, but in all, there are only two to four hanger servings per animal.

I would recommend giving the hanger a quick bash with a steak hammer or meat cleaver before cooking, not to flatten it, but just to break down some of the muscles that tighten up during cooking.

You only really want to cook this steak medium rare or rare, and be sure to give it a good rest in a warm, but not hot, place before serving. I would also suggest slicing the steak before serving – not so much for presentation but for ease of eating. This may all sound like hard work compared to other grilling steaks, but it's well worth the effort for a relatively cheap cut of meat.

This is the only beef cut that I serve off the bone, but I make up for that by accompanying it with a piece of stuffed and baked bone marrow shaft.

RIB STEAK

RUMP ON-THE-BONE

HANGER STEAK

RIB EDGE STEAK

RIB EDGE STEAK 350-400G

I'm always looking for new cuts on the bone and Peter Allen, our innovative butcher, has recently come up with this one. It's positioned on the flat chine bone on the rib. Usually the meat is stripped off the bone and diced when the popular rib eye cut is taken. You can either grill or roast it in a hot oven, then either slice the meat and lay it back on the bone or serve it still attached.

Cuts for slow-cooking

OXTAIL

A truly great cut for long, gentle cooking. Pieces of oxtail become meltingly tender on stewing, producing flavourful, gelatinous juices which thicken and enrich the cooking liquor. Your butcher will probably sell oxtail ready cut into pieces, but if not I'd recommend asking him to do so for you. Before cooking, trim off any excess fat from the meat, otherwise it will make the sauce greasy and you'll find it tricky to skim off all the fat from the surface after cooking. (See Braised oxtail with summer vegetables, page 151.)

SHORT RIBS

For a potential by-product, this is one of the most delicious braising cuts you can get your hands on. Braised slowly in liquor, short ribs are similar in texture and flavour to braised oxtail.

This cut is also known as Jacob's ladder, as the ribs do look rather like a ladder when they are left as a whole rack with the strips of meat intact between the rib bones. It is basically the bones and meat above the rib roast. Many butchers simply trim the meat between the bones and turn it into mince. But kept on the bone, in roughly 10cm lengths, and slowly braised – either as a rack or cut into pieces like spare ribs – it really does make a good all-round slow-cooking cut.

CROSS-CUT RIBS

I first came across this cut in a market in Baltimore, where street vendors were barbecueing cross-cut ribs seasoned with Cajun spices. I eventually persuaded our butcher Peter Allen, who is a dab hand at unusual cuts, to fathom it out for us.

it's basically a cut taken horizontally through a rack of short ribs or Jacob's ladder. Like short ribs, it makes a really interesting serving option for a relatively underused cut of beef that would normally go to mince or be used to make stock.

At the restaurant we brown these ribs, then slow-cook them in a barbecue sauce in the oven until tender (see recipe, page 152).

OXTAIL

SHORT RIBS

CROSS-CUT RIBS

VEAL

Thankfully there's an increasing number of producers in this country rearing veal calves for the table – either organically, or at least using acceptable farming practices. For years, veal has been shrouded by controversy, but this is largely down to the dubious Dutch crate production system, which involves rearing young calves in cruelly confined pens and feeding them an unnatural diet in order to keep their meat as pale as possible.

Rearing calves naturally to produce rosé veal is really no more reprehensible than producing spring lamb for the table. The term rosé is used to differentiate this type of veal, which, naturally, has a pink-red tinge. Rosé veal has a lot of other merits over its pale counterpart. It may not be quite as tender, but its flavour and texture are far superior and I think its darker colour makes it look a lot more inviting. The range of cuts is extensive too, offering plenty of flexibility in cooking. Any of the chops described below can be used for Grilled veal chop with offal salad on page 148.

Cuts for grilling

RIB CHOP 250-350G
This is the equivalent of a beef rib steak, cut from the rib end of the loin. It tends to cook up a little softer than its beef counterpart as it has a little more fat running through it. For me, a veal rib chop has a much better flavour and texture than a loin chop.

CUTLET 250-350G
Taken from the rack and/or best end, veal cutlets are presented with the chine bone removed and the bone is normally trimmed up. This is a great prime cut for grilling, as it has a good inner fat content and stays moist during grilling.

T-BONE 300-400G
Like the classic T-bone beef steak, this is a cut through the loin and tenderloin, effectively giving you two cuts in one.

LOIN CHOP 250-300G
Cut specifically from the loin, these chops may retain the chine bone as well as the main bone. They do not contain as much inner fat as cutlets and chops and therefore require careful cooking to ensure they don't dry out.

T-BONE

RIB CHOP

CUTLET

LOIN CHOP

SHIN

BREAST

Cuts for slow-cooking

SHIN

This is a classic braising cut, often sold under its familiar Italian name, *osso buco*, even in butchers' shops in this country. It is a cut taken straight across the shank and bone of the meatier hind leg of the animal – to give fairly generous slices, around 2–3cm thick.

Although a tougher braising cut, shin is not particularly economical because a calf's leg doesn't yield that many portions. Nevertheless, it is full of flavour, becomes deliciously tender with long, slow-cooking, and has the added advantage of succulent marrow rendered from the bone on braising. You may possibly need to order this cut, although most good butchers will have it.

BREAST

Typically boned, stuffed and rolled, this is an unusual cut to cook and serve on the bone, but it is excellent simply pot roasted or braised with herbs, fennel seeds and a flavourful stock. A breast of veal weighing around 1kg will serve two or three. (See also slow-roast breast of veal with onion and rosemary sauce, page 150.)

TAIL

Obviously calves tails are smaller than oxtails, but they can be cut into 2–3cm thick slices, trimmed of excess fat and braised in exactly the same way. This is another cut you may need to order in advance from your butcher.

TAIL

LAMB

Cooked on the bone, naturally reared British lamb is a lovely sweet meat and there are so many interesting cuts to choose from, apart from the obvious chops, cutlets, leg steaks etc. It's a real shame that butchers don't make much more of special breeds, like Portland, Blackface, Herdwick and Manx Loaghtan. These not only make a restaurant menu or butcher's counter look interesting, they each have a terrific, unique flavour of their own.

Other full-flavoured, naturally reared options are Saltmarsh lamb from animals that graze on the drained Romney Marshes in Kent, and Shetland lamb from lambs that feed naturally on the island's sea-washed pastures, heather-clad hillsides and seaweed from the shores.

I'm still flying the flag for mutton at the restaurant too. It's an obvious choice for casseroles, hotpots and meaty broths, where a real depth of flavour is needed. And when we make a mutton chop curry it literally flies out of the kitchen.

Cuts for grilling

BARNSLEY CHOP 250-350G

Sometimes referred to as a saddle chop, this is my favourite lamb cut for grilling. It is cut across the saddle, producing a double loin chop, which includes the little under fillet all in one.

Apparently this chop originated in the Kings Head pub in Barnsley in 1849 to provide a substantial lunch for local farmers. The chops were also served at the celebration of the opening of Barnsley town hall in 1933.

These chops shouldn't have too much fat on them, as the fat is difficult to render down during cooking, so trim away any excess beforehand. Along with cutlets, a Barnsley chop is probably the most consistent lamb chop as it is cut from the prime joint.

CHUMP CHOP 120-150G

The chump is cut from the rump at the end of the saddle, so it is positioned between the loin and the leg. It has a great flavour and some butchers are now selling whole chumps as a small roasting joint to serve two. Chump chops won't be quite as tender as cutlets or Barnsley chops, but they will certainly taste very good.

CUTLET 70-100G

Cutlets are the most highly regarded chops on the beast and you will pay a premium for them. Many butchers and chefs trim them far too much for my liking, sometimes stripping every little bit of fat back to the eye of the meat. I like to leave the fat on, right up the end of the bone, as it is sweet and delicious – provided the cutlets are grilled properly until the fat is really crisp. Allow three cutlets per portion, depending on size.

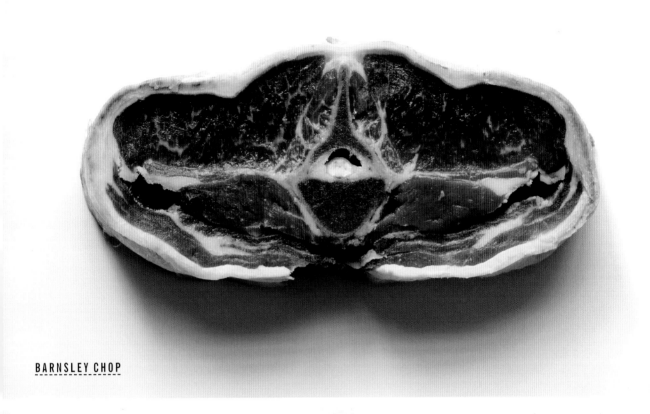

BARNSLEY CHOP

CHUMP CHOP

CUTLET

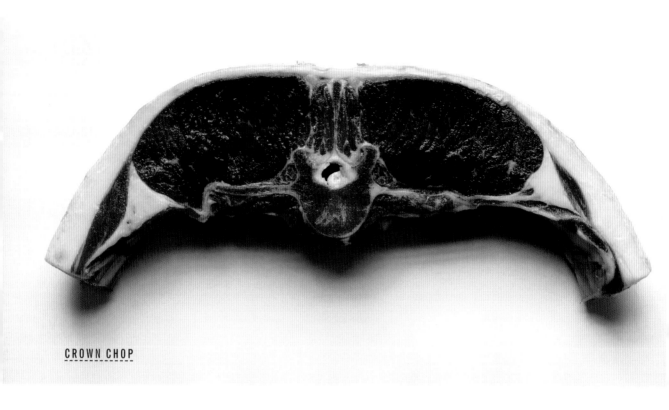

CROWN CHOP

LEG STEAK

LOIN CHOP

CROWN CHOP 180-220G

This is a double lamb cutlet, akin to a Barnsley chop, but cut from the best end rather than the loin. It isn't a cut you'll commonly find at the butcher's, but we sometimes have it on the menu as it has a fine flavour and is meltingly tender if cooked properly. Some butchers do refer to the Barnsley chop as a crown chop, so it does get a bit confusing.

LEG STEAK 250-350G

A leg steak is cut straight across the leg through the bone and is 1–2cm thick. Leg steaks for grilling, frying or barbecueing are best appreciated from new season's lamb, as those taken from an older animal can be a bit on the tough side.

LOIN CHOP 120-160G

As their name suggest, these chops are from the loin and they incorporate the small under fillet. Suitable for frying, grilling or barbecueing, they have a good flavour and texture. (See Lamb chops with cucumber and mint, page 148.) Every high street butcher sells loin chops, sometimes mixed in with other chops cut from along the saddle and best end.

SCRAG END OF NECK

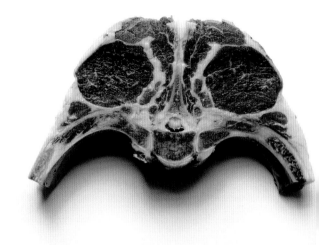

MIDDLE NECK

SHANK

MUTTON CHOP

SHOULDER

Cuts for slow-cooking

SCRAG END OF NECK
Taken from the head end of the animal, this is a tougher cut with a fair amount of connective tissue, and a full flavour. It's ideal for stewing and braising. I like to use this part of the neck cut into slices, with the bone in the centre – you'll need one or two slices per serving. Long, slow-cooking renders this neck cut very tender.

MIDDLE NECK
Taken from just below the scrag end, this cut has the appearance of a double chop. It is the perfect choice for a hotpot or a straightforward braise, as the meat around the neck is quite heavily marbled with fat and therefore stays moist and tender during slow-cooking.

SHOULDER
A cut through the shoulder bone, weighing about 800g is perfect for two. Just get your butcher to saw through the meatiest end of the shoulder, right through the blade bone. Either roast slowly in the oven with herbs and spices or confit in duck fat.

SHANK
This is basically the knuckle end of the leg, which is typically left on if it is to be roasted, or often minced or diced for stewing meat by the butcher. Whole lamb shanks are also delicious cuts for slow-cooking in their own right. A few years back, you couldn't go to a pub or restaurant without seeing a braised lamb shank in some form on the menu; as a consequence, it has lost some of its appeal. That said, it is a great, flavourful braising cut and at least restaurants have managed to raise its profile.

MUTTON CHOP
Mutton chops – cut from the loin, best end or the chump of older animals – are great for slow-cooked dishes such as Irish stew, Lancashire hotpot or a mutton chop curry like the one we serve in the restaurant (see recipe, page 144).

PORK

The rare breed pig revival has gathered momentum in this country and there are some serious pig farmers around the country like Peter Gott up in Cumbria, who breeds Tamworths, Middle Whites and Saddleworths among others. Peter has reintroduced many forgotten breeds and rears an array of cross-breeds, including his trademark wild boar and Iron Age.

Naturally reared pigs have more fat marbling through their meat and individual cuts have a good layer of covering fat, but don't let this put you off. The fat is a great source of flavour, it helps to keep the meat moist during cooking, and anyway some of it will melt away during cooking. It goes without saying that the meat is far tastier than anything from a commercially reared pig. Thankfully names such as Gloucestershire Old Spot and Saddleworth are becoming familiar now that we are accustomed to seeing quality pork named by breed on restaurant menus.

Cuts for grilling

BARON CHOP 500-600G FOR 2
This is basically a pork version of a Barnsley lamb chop – a double loin chop. Obviously it comes up larger and is great for two or three people to share. Best simply grilled or roasted.

T-BONE 300-400G
As the name suggests, this cut – through the loin and tenderloin fillet – is like a T-bone beef steak. It's a nice way of getting two different textured meats in one cut.

CUTLET 250-300G
Butchers rarely differentiate between cutlets (or rib chops) and loin chops, in the way that they do with beef and lamb, but it is worth specifying that you would like a chop cut from the foreloin or rib end if you prefer a bit more fat running through your chop. The extra fat keeps a rib chop more moist during cooking.

LOIN CHOP 250-300G
Loin, like a sirloin of beef, has less fat and the chops therefore need careful cooking to keep them moist.

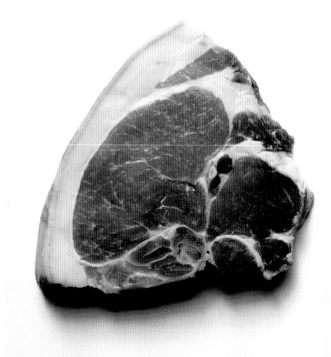

T-BONE

124

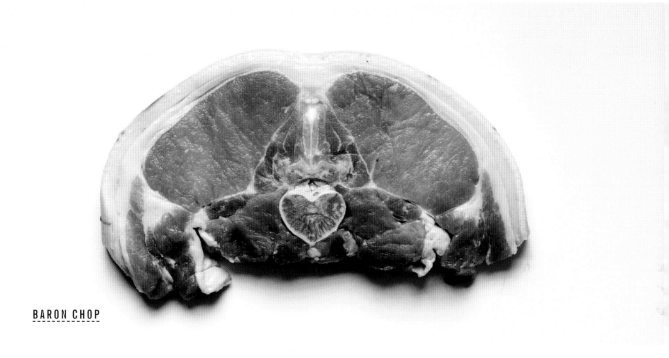

BARON CHOP

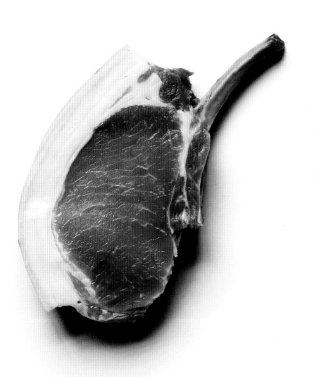

CUTLET

LOIN CHOP

BELLY

Cuts for slow-cooking

BELLY

This has become the chef's preferred pork cut. You can serve pork belly on or off the bone, though we naturally keep the bone in place during slow-cooking. Cooking time varies and you may or may not need to trim the rind and some fat off prior to cooking, depending on the breed and fat covering. A 1kg piece of belly will serve two or three.

NECK CHOP

Neck chops are really flavoursome and well suited to slow-cooking. Although not as tender as the chops from the loin, they may sometimes be alright to grill.

PORK KNUCKLE

This is quite a humble cut but it has a fantastic flavour. Suitable for roasting or slow roasting, one knuckle will serve two or three. Try baking a dish of sliced potatoes and apples, finishing the pork for the last 45 minutes or so on top of the potatoes.

NECK CHOP

PORK KNUCKLE

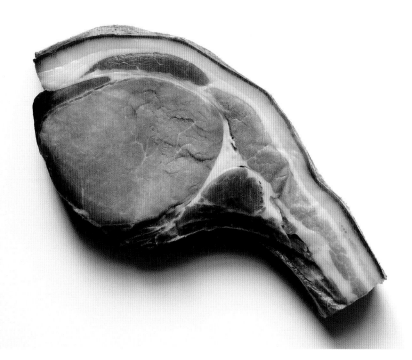

BACON CHOP

Ham and bacon

HAM HOCK

This is probably the most flavoursome of all the ham joints and makes tasty stock for a hearty split pea soup. It can be simply boiled with an onion, carrot, some peppercorns and thyme sprigs, then served either hot with a creamy parsley sauce, or cold with mustard and pickles.

BACON CHOP

If your butcher cures his bacon on the bone then this back bacon chop makes an interesting cut. You can, of course, prepare your own if you're into home-curing. Bacon chops are suitable for grilling, pan-frying or even slow-cooking.

BACON STREAKY CHOP

We normally soak this chop in cold water for a while before cooking, as it has a tendency to be salty. Grill, pan-fry or slow-cook.

HAM HOCK

BACON STREAKY CHOP

VENISON

Venison is a generic term, covering different species of deer, including the roe deer, red deer, fallow and muntjac, all of which vary in size and do have different eating qualities. The meat from a roe deer, for example, is rather more tender than that from a red deer. The flavour also varies significantly according to how long the carcass has been hung for.

Not many butchers take the time to break down a venison carcass in the way they would a lamb, which I can never understand as it would provide more value for the butcher and more variety for the customer. As you can see, the cuts here are pretty similar to those from a lamb carcass. Of course, if you live in the country and you're able to buy large portions of meat carcasses direct from a local farmer, you might like to have a go at butchery, preparing some of these cuts yourself.

CUTLET 60-80G
This is quite a fancy cut of venison and it's pretty expensive, but if you are out to impress it is a fine-looking cut. It takes very little time to cook and can be simply pan-fried or grilled. Allow three cutlets per portion, depending on size.

Venison cutlets can be treated in exactly the same way as lamb cutlets, but when cooking, do bear in mind that venison meat is very lean and therefore less forgiving.

A good butcher or game dealer will break the carcass down into chops and cutlets, though often the loin is simply stripped out, which is a shame because venison chops and cutlets are interesting cuts to cook with.

LOIN CHOP 90-100G
This can be cut from any part of the saddle and – like a lamb chop – it will sometimes include the under fillet, depending on which particular part of the saddle it is cut from. A loin chop will be more economical than a cutlet, though again you may have difficulty in persuading your butcher to offer venison loin chops.

BARNSLEY CHOP 200-250G
This is a cut across the saddle, like a Barnsley lamb chop. Sadly, few butchers and game dealers will go to the trouble of cutting these, but it's worth asking.

RACK
This can be treated just like a rack of lamb and either roasted or grilled whole and carved into individual cutlets before serving. One four-rib half-rack is a convenient size to serve two.

SHANK
This is a lovely and unusual cut for slow-cooking. It is best braised and can be treated in the same way as a lamb shank. Again, this is a cut you may need to request specifically from your butcher.

SHANK

RACK

CUTLET

LOIN CHOP

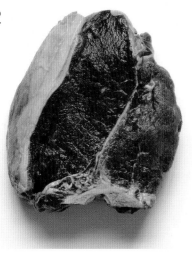

BARNSLEY CHOP

SAUCES AND BUTTERS FOR GRILLED MEATS

Accompaniments for grilled meats are quite a personal thing. I sometimes find myself craving for bearnaise sauce to go with grilled meat or fish – and to dunk my chips into. At other times I just fancy a bit of mustard and a nice, clean green salad. I'm not big on sauces, especially with quality cuts of meat, but some really suit a particular dish if you're in the mood.

GREEN SAUCE

This is rather like an Italian salsa verde. It is excellent served with simple grilled meats, mixed grills and robust grilled fish.

Serves 4

30g mint leaves

30g parsley leaves

30g basil leaves

30g capers, rinsed

1 garlic clove, peeled and crushed, or a few wild garlic leaves

2 tsp Tewkesbury or English mustard

about 100ml cold-pressed rapeseed oil

sea salt and freshly ground black pepper

Put the herb leaves, capers, garlic and mustard into a blender with most of the rapeseed oil and process to a fairly course purée. Season with salt and pepper to taste and add a little more oil if the sauce seems a little dry.

CHOP HOUSE BUTTER

This is a simpler, British version of the famous Café de Paris butter, which has no end of flavouring ingredients added in. Serve it on grilled steaks and chops.

Makes 300g

1 tbsp cold-pressed rapeseed oil

1 red onion, peeled and finely chopped

1 garlic clove, peeled and crushed

1 tsp coarsely ground black pepper

½ tbsp thyme leaves, chopped

½ tbsp freshly grated horseradish

100ml red wine

250g butter, softened

1 tbsp Henderson's Relish or Worcestershire sauce

1 tbsp HP sauce

1 tbsp Tewkesbury or English mustard

1 tsp Gentleman's Relish

2 tbsp chopped parsley

½ tbsp chopped tarragon

Heat the rapeseed oil in a pan and add the onion, garlic and pepper. Cook gently for 2–3 minutes to soften, then tip into a bowl. Add all of the other ingredients and mix well.

Spoon the flavoured butter onto a sheet of cling film or greaseproof paper and shape into a cylinder, about 3cm in diameter, sealing it in the film or paper. Refrigerate or freeze until required.

Just slice the chilled butter as you need it and serve directly on steaks and chops; or cut off as much frozen butter as you need and slice it before serving.

BEARNAISE SAUCE

This is the classic sauce to accompany grilled meats and fish. It's not a British sauce as such, but you can bet your life if you don't serve it the customer will ask for it.

Serves 4–6

1 tbsp white wine or cider vinegar

1 small shallot, peeled and roughly chopped

a few sprigs of tarragon, leaves picked, stalks reserved

a few sprigs of chervil, leaves picked, stalks reserved

5 black peppercorns

200g unsalted butter

3 small egg yolks

salt and freshly ground white pepper

a little lemon juice (optional)

Put the vinegar, 2 tbsp water, the shallot, herb stalks and peppercorns in a saucepan and simmer for a minute or until the liquid has reduced to 2 tsp. Strain through a sieve and leave to cool.

Melt the butter in a saucepan over a low heat and let bubble very gently for 3–4 minutes. Remove from the heat, leave to cool a little, then pour off the pure liquid butter into a bowl, leaving the milky whey behind. Discard the whey. (Clarifying the butter in this way helps to keep the sauce thick.)

Put the egg yolks into a small heatproof bowl (or a double boiler if you have one) with half of the vinegar reduction and set over a pan of gently simmering water. Whisk the mixture until it begins to thicken and become frothy. Slowly trickle in two-thirds of the clarified butter, whisking continuously – preferably using an electric hand whisk. If the butter is added too quickly, the sauce is liable to separate.

Now taste the sauce and add a little more, or all, of the remaining vinegar reduction. Then whisk in the rest of the butter. The vinegar should just cut the oiliness of the butter sauce; don't add too much. Season with salt and pepper to taste.

Cover the bowl and leave in a warm, not hot, place until needed, but no longer than 20 minutes.

To serve, chop the tarragon and chervil leaves and stir into the sauce. Check the seasoning and add a squeeze of lemon juice, to taste. Whisk lightly.

WILD GARLIC SAUCE

A delicious sauce to serve with grilled meats, and roast poultry and game. When wild garlic is in season, it's handy to purée some in a blender with a little oil and store it in a sealed jar in the fridge topped with a film of oil. Alternatively, you can blend it with a little water and freeze the purée in little tubs.

Serves 4

2–3 handfuls of wild garlic leaves, washed and dried

1–2 tsp Tewkesbury or English mustard

100–150ml cold-pressed rapeseed oil

salt and freshly ground black pepper

Put the wild garlic leaves, mustard and 100ml rapeseed oil into a blender and process as smoothly or as coarsely as you wish. Season with salt and pepper to taste. Add as much of the extra oil as you need to get the desired consistency.

BAKED NEW SEASON'S GARLIC SAUCE

I like to serve this with roast chicken when new season's garlic is available during the spring (see page 134). Bake the garlic alongside the chicken.

Serves 4

4 heads of new season's garlic
a few sprigs of curly parsley
½ tbsp Dijon mustard, or more to taste
2–3 tbsp duck fat, warmed (or pan juices from a roasted chicken)
70g fresh white breadcrumbs
a little milk to mix
sea salt and freshly ground black pepper

Preheat the oven to 200°C/gas mark 6. Wrap the garlic bulbs in foil and bake them in the oven for 1 hour. Unwrap and leave until cool enough to handle, then peel away any tough outer skin.

Put the garlic into a blender with the parsley, mustard, warm duck fat (or chicken pan juices) and breadcrumbs and blend until smooth. Add enough milk to give the sauce a thick pouring consistency and season with salt and pepper to taste.

CHOP HOUSE SAUCE

This slightly piquant sauce goes really well with simple grilled pork, bacon or veal; we serve it with a breaded flattened pork cutlet too.

Serves 4

a couple of knobs of butter
1 small onion, peeled and finely chopped
1 garlic clove, peeled and crushed
a good pinch of cayenne pepper
1 tsp plain flour
½ tsp tomato purée
1 tbsp cider vinegar
1 tsp redcurrant jelly
1 tsp English mustard
250ml hot beef stock
salt and freshly ground black pepper
1 large dill pickle or a few gherkins, finely diced

Melt the butter in a heavy-based pan and add the onion, garlic and cayenne pepper. Cook gently for 2–3 minutes to soften, then stir in the flour, followed by the tomato purée, cider vinegar, redcurrant jelly and mustard.

Gradually whisk in the hot beef stock, bring to the boil and season lightly with salt and pepper. Simmer very gently for about 15 minutes (a simmer plate or heat-diffuser mat is useful here). Add the dill pickle and re-season if necessary. The sauce should be quite thick, if not continue simmering a little longer.

ROAST CHICKEN WITH NEW SEASON'S GARLIC SAUCE

This dish was inspired by several visits to L'amis Louis in Paris, where the food is simple and honest, respecting the quality ingredients used. We buy traditionally reared Woolley Park Farm chickens, which have an amazing gamey flavour.

Serves 3–4

1 free-range chicken, about 1.5kg, with livers
sea salt and freshly ground black pepper
a few sprigs each of thyme and rosemary
a few generous knobs of butter

For the stuffing
60g butter
1 medium onion, peeled and finely chopped
100g chicken livers, chopped
2 tsp thyme leaves
80–100g fresh white breadcrumbs
2 tbsp chopped parsley

To serve
a little chopped parsley
Baked new season's garlic sauce (page 133)
Straw potatoes (page 164)

Preheat the oven to 200°C/gas mark 6. Season the chicken inside and out. Put the herbs into the cavity. Rub butter all over the breast and legs.

For the stuffing, melt the butter in a pan. Add the onion, livers and thyme, season and cook over a medium heat for 2–3 minutes. Off the heat, mix in the breadcrumbs, parsley and seasoning. Either use to stuff your bird or cook separately in an ovenproof dish or wrapped in foil for the last 30–40 minutes.

Put the chicken into a large roasting tin and roast in the oven, basting regularly and adding the livers to the roasting tin for the last 6 minutes or so. Test the chicken after 1¼ hours by inserting a skewer into the thickest part of the thigh. The juices should run clear; if not roast for a little longer.

Lift the chicken onto a warmed platter and rest in a warm place for 15 minutes. Sprinkle with chopped parsley and serve with the roasted livers, stuffing, garlic sauce and straw potatoes.

CHICKEN AND LOBSTER PIE

This is a bit of a take on my rabbit and crayfish pie that was successful on BBC2's Great British Menu a few years back. Shellfish like lobster and prawns really do go well with the delicate flavour of chicken. For slow-cooked chicken dishes I use thighs rather than breast meat as they stay more moist and succulent.

Serves 4

2 cooked lobsters, about 500g each
500g boned and skinned free-range chicken thighs
1 tbsp chopped parsley
½ tbsp chopped tarragon leaves
350–400g ready-made all-butter puff pastry
plain flour for dusting
1 free-range egg, beaten

For the lobster sauce
1 tbsp vegetable oil
reserved lobster shells
4 shallots, peeled and roughly chopped
1 garlic clove, peeled and chopped
60g butter
60g plain flour
a good pinch of saffron strands
a few sprigs of tarragon
½ tbsp tomato purée
60ml white wine
500ml hot fish stock
500ml hot chicken stock
400ml double cream
salt and freshly ground black pepper
1–2 tsp cornflour (if needed)

Remove the meat from the lobster tails and claws and cut roughly into 1cm pieces. Reserve one lobster head (if making a large pie). Break the rest of the shells up a bit, using a heavy knife. Cut the chicken thighs in half, or into thirds if large. Cover and refrigerate the lobster and chicken meat.

To make the sauce, heat the oil in a heavy-based saucepan and fry the lobster shells, shallots and garlic over a medium heat for about 5 minutes until they begin to colour lightly. Add the butter and, once melted, stir in the flour. Add the saffron, tarragon and tomato purée, then gradually stir in the white wine and the hot fish and chicken stocks.

Bring to the boil, lower the heat and simmer for about 30 minutes until the sauce has reduced by about half, then add the cream. Season lightly with salt and pepper, bring back to the boil and simmer very gently for about 20 minutes until the sauce has reduced by half again. (A simmer plate or heat-diffuser mat is useful here.)

Strain the sauce through a colander into a clean pan, moving the shells with a spoon to ensure all the sauce goes through.

Tip about one-tenth of the shells into a blender and add about a cupful of the strained sauce. Blend until smooth, then strain through a fine-meshed sieve into the sauce in the pan.

Bring the sauce back to the boil, add the chicken and simmer for 5 minutes. The sauce should be a thick coating consistency by now; if not, simmer a little longer (or dilute a little cornflour in water and stir into the sauce). Leave to cool.

Stir the lobster and chopped parsley and tarragon into the cooled sauce. Adjust the seasoning if necessary. Fill a large pie dish or 4 individual ones with the mixture.

Roll out the pastry on a lightly floured surface to a 5mm thickness. Trim to about 2cm larger all round than the pie dish (or cut discs large enough to cover individual dishes). Brush the edges of the pastry with a little of the beaten egg. Lay the pastry over the filling, pressing the egg-washed sides onto the rim of the dish(es).

If making a large pie, cut a cross in the centre and insert the reserved lobster head, so it sits proud. Cut a small slit in the top of individual pies to allow steam to escape. Leave to rest in a cool place for 30 minutes.

Preheat the oven to 200°C/gas mark 6. Brush the pastry lid with beaten egg and bake the pie for 40–50 minutes or until golden brown (allow 10–15 minutes less for individual pies). Let the pie stand for a few minutes before serving.

DUCK HASH WITH A FRIED DUCK'S EGG

I first had duck hash at Herbsaint, a great restaurant in New Orleans. It seemed a brilliant idea, so I came up with my own version, which we serve for brunch, lunch and dinner.

Serves 4

4 medium duck legs

½ head of garlic

sea salt and freshly ground black pepper

a bouquet garni (2 bay leaves, a few sprigs of thyme, ½ tbsp each coriander seeds and white peppercorns, 5 cloves, ¼ cinnamon stick and 10 crushed juniper berries, tied together in muslin)

250–300g duck fat, melted

2 medium onions, peeled and roughly diced

350g new potatoes, peeled and cooked

1 tbsp Worcestershire sauce, or to taste

2–3 tbsp cold-pressed rapeseed oil

2 tbsp fresh white breadcrumbs

4 duck's eggs

Preheat the oven to 160°C/gas mark 3. Place the duck legs in a heavy-based ovenproof pan in which they fit snugly and scatter over the garlic and 1½ tsp sea salt. Add the muslin bag of herbs and spices. Pour the duck fat over the duck legs to cover them. Slowly bring to a simmer, then put the lid on.

Transfer to the oven and cook for about 1½ hours until the meat is just coming away from the bone. Leave to cool for an hour, then take out the duck legs. Strain the fat into a jar (store in the fridge).

Heat a spoonful of duck fat in a heavy-based pan and add the onions. Cover and cook for 5–6 minutes until soft and lightly coloured. Tip into a bowl.

Cut the cooked potatoes roughly into 1cm chunks. Heat another 1 tbsp duck fat in a heavy-based frying pan until very hot. Fry the potatoes in batches over a high heat until lightly coloured. Drain and add to the onions. Strip the meat from the duck legs and cut into rough 1cm chunks with the skin. Add to the potatoes and mix well, seasoning and adding Worcestershire sauce to taste.

Divide the mixture into 4 portions and shape into patties, about 8cm in diameter. Refrigerate for a couple of hours or overnight.

Coat the patties all over with breadcrumbs. Heat 1–2 tbsp rapeseed oil in a non-stick frying pan and fry the patties for 3–4 minutes on each side until golden and crisp. Keep warm in the oven.

Heat 1–2 tbsp oil in a frying pan and gently fry the duck's eggs for a couple of minutes, seasoning the whites lightly. Place a duck hash patty on each warmed plate, slide a fried egg on top and serve.

RABBIT AND GIROLLES ON GRILLED PUFFBALL

If you have braised some rabbit legs or made a pie, then this is a great way to use the saddle fillets and offal – and enjoy the pick of our wild mushrooms.

Serves 4

vegetable or corn oil for brushing

4 slices of puffball, about 1.5cm thick

8 rabbit saddle fillets

hearts and liver from 4 rabbits

salt and freshly ground black pepper

100ml red wine

120g butter

120–150g girolles or chanterelles, cleaned

2 tbsp chopped parsley

Heat a ridged griddle pan or heavy-based frying pan and lightly oil it. Cook the puffball for 2–3 minutes on each side, then remove and keep warm.

Meanwhile, season the rabbit fillets and offal. Cook them in the same pan, adding a little more oil if necessary, for 2–3 minutes on each side, keeping them nice and pink. Remove and keep warm.

Add the wine to the pan to deglaze with about 30g of the butter, then pour off into a small jug.

Heat the rest of the butter in a frying pan until foaming. Add the mushrooms and parsley, season and cook very briefly for about 30 seconds, turning them as they cook.

To serve, place a puffball slice on each warmed plate. Cut each saddle fillet into 3 or 4 slices and arrange on the puffball with the offal. Scatter the girolles and butter on top and spoon the pan juices around. Serve at once.

MIXED GRILL OF PORK WITH CRAB APPLE SAUCE

A few years ago I bought some lovely metal skewers (pictured) from my favourite cookshop in Paris – E Dehillerin in rue Coquillière. They are perfect for this robust pork dish, which we serve on bespoke wooden boards with grooves to catch the juices.

This recipe involves lots of different bits of the pig, but you can really use whatever cuts and offal you fancy. It's a great way to cook rare breed pork from farms that sell their meat by the quarter beast, as Richard Vaughan of Huntsham Farm in Herefordshire does with his Middle White pork.

Of course you can always cook some pork crackling (see page 33) to add to the platters. If you haven't got access to crab apples then make the sauce with Bramleys instead.

Serves 4

150g minced pork (with about 20% fat)
100g black pudding, finely chopped
salt and freshly ground black pepper
200–250g pork loin fillet or tenderloin
200–250g shoulder or neck fillet of pork
2 pig's kidneys, trimmed
150g pig's liver
vegetable oil for brushing
a generous knob of butter
a few sprigs of rosemary

For the crab apple sauce
300–350g crab apples
1 tbsp caster sugar, or more to taste

First make the crab apple sauce. Remove the stalks from the apples and wash them well. Put them into a heavy-based saucepan with 1 tbsp sugar, cover and cook for 10–15 minutes, stirring every so often until the apples are soft. If there's a lot of liquid, remove the lid and boil rapidly until it dries out enough, taking care that it doesn't splatter. Transfer to a bowl and taste for sweetness, adding a little more sugar if needed. Spoon into individual serving bowls and let cool to room temperature.

In a bowl, mix the minced pork with the black pudding and season well with salt and pepper. Divide into 4 portions, flatten and shape into patties. Cover and place in the fridge. Cut the pork loin into 4 similar-sized chunks; do the same with the pork shoulder, kidneys and liver. Season all of the meat.

Heat a ridged griddle pan or heavy-based frying pan and lightly oil it. Cook the pork patties and pieces of meat and offal in batches as necessary, for about 3–4 minutes on each side, keeping them slightly pink. The liver and kidney will need less time, just 1–2 minutes.

Heat the butter and rosemary in a separate pan until foaming and remove from the heat. Thread the meat onto skewers or simply arrange on warmed plates. Trickle the butter over the meat and serve, with the crab apple sauce.

HAM HOCK WITH PEASE PUDDING AND TEWKESBURY MUSTARD SAUCE

This is old-fashioned cooking at its best. Your butcher should be able to supply you with some ham hocks or knuckles relatively cheaply. They have a fantastic flavour and once cooked, you'll have a flavourful stock base for a soup. Use any leftover meat in salads, soups and sandwiches.

Serves 4

4 small unsmoked ham hocks or knuckles, about 800g each, soaked overnight in cold water to remove any excess salt

1 onion, peeled and roughly chopped

2 carrots, peeled and roughly chopped

1 bay leaf

5 cloves

1 tsp black peppercorns

120g dried yellow split peas, soaked overnight in cold water

a generous knob of butter

salt and freshly ground white pepper

For the mustard sauce

30g butter

2 large shallots, peeled and finely chopped

20g plain flour

1 tbsp Tewkesbury mustard, or more to taste

300ml ham cooking liquor

2 tbsp double cream

1 tbsp chopped parsley

Drain the ham hocks, rinse in cold water and put them into a large cooking pot with the onion, carrots, bay leaf, cloves and peppercorns. Add enough cold water to cover generously and bring to the boil. Skim off any scum from the surface and simmer gently, covered, for 1 hour.

Drain the split peas, tie them loosely in a piece of muslin and add to the cooking pot. Top up with more water if necessary. Continue to simmer for another hour, then lift out the bag of peas and check that they have turned into a chunky purée by pressing the bag between your fingers. Check the hocks as well to see whether the meat is tender and coming away from the bone. If either the meat or peas are not quite ready, simmer for a little longer.

To make the sauce, melt the butter in a heavy-based pan and add the shallots. Cook gently over a low heat for a few minutes until soft. Add the flour and mustard and cook, stirring, for a minute, then gradually add 300ml of the ham liquor, stirring with a whisk to avoid lumps. Bring to the boil and season with a little salt and pepper.

Simmer the sauce for about 20 minutes, stirring every so often. It should be quite thick by now; if not, simmer a little longer. Stir in the cream and parsley. Taste and adjust the seasoning if necessary and add a little more mustard if you think it is needed. Simmer for another minute or so; keep warm.

Once the ham hocks are cool enough to handle, lift them out of the pan, reserving the liquor, and cut off the outer layer of fat with a knife. Carefully remove the smaller bone by twisting and pulling it out, leaving the larger bone attached. (If the hocks are a bit large you can cut off some of the meat at this stage for a salad, soup or sandwiches if you like.)

To serve, reheat the ham hocks in the reserved cooking liquor. Meanwhile, reheat the pease pudding with the butter, adding a little water if it seems too thick. Season with pepper to taste and a little salt if needed.

Drain the ham hocks and place in warmed deep plates with a portion of pease pudding. Spoon the mustard sauce over the meat and serve.

MUTTON CHOP CURRY

The Oyster & Chop House menu wouldn't be the same without a mutton chop or halibut collar curry. For some reason, most restaurants and butchers struggle to sell mutton but we can't seem to cook enough of it. Out of the traditional mutton breed season, we use Blackface or Herdwick, which have different lambing seasons.

Make a quantity of the roasted curry spices as below and keep in a sealed jar – you'll have enough for a few batches of curry.

For the roasted curry spice mix

1 tbsp fenugreek seeds

1 tbsp fennel seeds

1 tbsp fenugreek leaves

1 tbsp cumin seeds

1–2 tbsp dried chilli flakes

½ tbsp caraway seeds

½ tbsp nigella seeds

1 tbsp turmeric

8 cloves

1 tbsp mustard seeds

½ tbsp cardamom seeds (from green cardamom pods)

1 tbsp ground cumin

1 tsp ground cinnamon

1 tbsp ground coriander

To prepare the spice mix, grind all of the spices, except the ground cumin, cinnamon and coriander, in a spice grinder or with a mortar and pestle. Then mix them with the ready-ground spices and sprinkle into a heavy-based frying pan. Cook over a medium heat, stirring constantly, until they turn dark brown; don't let them burn. Tip onto a plate and leave to cool, then store in a sealed jar until needed.

Serves 4

For the curry

12 mutton chops or cutlets

2–3 tbsp natural yoghurt

75g ghee (or half oil, half butter mix)

2 medium red onions, peeled and finely chopped

3 garlic cloves, peeled and crushed

a small piece of fresh root ginger, peeled and finely grated

a good pinch of saffron strands

a good handful of curry leaves

2 tbsp roasted curry spice mix (see left)

1 tbsp tomato purée

500ml lamb or beef stock

salt and freshly ground black pepper

a few sprigs of coriander, roughly chopped

1 tbsp vegetable oil

Coat the mutton chops with the yoghurt and leave to marinate for a couple of hours.

Meanwhile, heat two-thirds of the ghee in a pan and gently cook the onions with the garlic, ginger, saffron and a few of the curry leaves for 3–4 minutes until softened. Add the roasted curry spice mix and tomato purée and stir well. Pour in the stock and bring to the boil, then lower the heat and let the sauce simmer for 20 minutes.

Transfer the sauce to a blender and process until smooth, then strain through a fine-meshed sieve into a clean pan, pushing as much through as possible. Return to a low heat and simmer until the sauce has reduced and thickened.

Heat the remaining ghee in a frying pan. Remove excess yoghurt from the chops and season them, then fry until lightly coloured on both sides. Pour the sauce over the chops and simmer gently for 15–20 minutes, stirring occasionally. Add the coriander and simmer for another couple of minutes.

Meanwhile, heat the oil in a frying pan and briefly fry the rest of the curry leaves. Scatter over the curry and serve with basmati rice.

LAMB'S SWEETBREADS WITH RUNNER BEANS, BACON AND MUSHROOMS

This is a lovely light main course, or you could serve smaller portions as a starter. Try to buy the plumper sweetbreads from above the heart if you possibly can, as those of the thymus glands in the neck can be a little scraggy.

Serves 4

300–400g lamb's sweetbreads

salt and freshly ground black pepper

250–300g runner beans, trimmed

100g butter

120g piece of unsmoked streaky bacon, cut into 5mm dice

150g girolles or other seasonal wild mushrooms, cleaned

1 tbsp cold-pressed rapeseed oil

For the dressing

1 small red onion, peeled and finely chopped

3 tbsp cider vinegar

1 tsp Tewkesbury mustard

4 tbsp cold-pressed rapeseed oil

Put the sweetbreads into a pan of cold salted water, bring to the boil and lower the heat. Simmer for 2–3 minutes, then drain and leave to cool.

Meanwhile, for the dressing, put the red onion, cider vinegar and 2 tbsp water into a small pan and simmer for 2–3 minutes or until the liquid has reduced by half. Remove from the heat and whisk in the mustard and rapeseed oil. Season with salt and pepper and set aside.

Shred the runner beans lengthways on a slight angle very finely. Add to a saucepan of boiling salted water and cook for 30 seconds, then drain in a colander. Refresh briefly under the cold tap, drain and pat dry with kitchen paper.

Trim the blanched sweetbreads of any fat and membrane, then season them. Melt half the butter in a frying pan and cook the sweetbreads, stirring frequently, over a fairly high heat for 4–5 minutes until golden. Drain on kitchen paper and keep warm.

Melt the rest of the butter in the frying pan. Add the bacon pieces and fry over a medium heat for 2–3 minutes, then add the mushrooms. Cook for 4–5 minutes until tender, turning them every so often and lightly seasoning them.

Meanwhile, warm the runner beans in 1 tbsp rapeseed oil, then toss in the dressing and season.

To serve, divide the runner beans between warmed serving plates and scatter the sweetbreads and mushrooms over the top. Serve at once.

GRILLED VEAL CHOP WITH OFFAL SALAD

British veal is well worth a try. Serving the offal in a leafy salad alongside makes the chops that much more interesting.

Serves 4

200–250g veal offal, such as liver, kidney, heart, sweetbreads, trimmed

4 veal chops or cutlets, about 300g each

salt and freshly ground black pepper

vegetable or corn oil for brushing

2 tbsp cold-pressed rapeseed oil

a couple of good knobs of butter

a couple of handfuls of small tasty salad leaves, such as pea shoots, buckler leaf sorrel, rocket, purslane, washed

Tewkesbury mustard dressing (page 55)

Cut the offal into 1cm chunks and set aside.

Heat a ridged griddle pan or heavy-based frying pan. Season the veal chops with salt and pepper and brush with oil. Cook for about 5 minutes on each side, depending on thickness, keeping them nice and pink.

Meanwhile, heat the rapeseed oil in a heavy-based frying pan. Add the butter and heat until foaming, then season the offal pieces and add them to the pan. Fry briskly over a high heat for 2–3 minutes until nicely coloured, but keeping them pink in the middle. Remove from the pan and put to one side.

While the offal is cooking, toss the salad leaves with the dressing in a bowl. Add the offal, toss briefly and arrange on serving plates alongside the chops.

LAMB CHOPS WITH CUCUMBER AND MINT

Cooking cucumbers may seem a bit odd, but it's really no different to cooking courgettes or marrow and I reckon they have more flavour.

Serves 4

2 cucumbers

8 lamb loin chops, about 120–150g each

salt and freshly ground black pepper

vegetable or corn oil for brushing

2 tbsp cold-pressed rapeseed oil

2 large shallots, peeled, halved and thinly sliced

a small handful of mint leaves, shredded

Cut the cucumbers in half lengthways and scoop out the seeds with a teaspoon. Cut each half on an angle into 1–2cm thick slices.

Heat a ridged griddle pan or heavy-based frying pan over a medium-high heat. Season the lamb chops with salt and pepper, brush with oil and cook for about 5 minutes on each side, keeping them pink.

Meanwhile, heat the rapeseed oil in another frying pan and add the shallots. Fry, stirring, for a minute, then add the cucumber slices. Season with salt and pepper and sauté over a fairly high heat for 2–3 minutes until tender. Take off the heat and stir in the shredded mint.

Divide the cucumber between warmed plates and place the lamb chops on top to serve.

SLOW-ROAST BREAST OF VEAL WITH ONION AND ROSEMARY SAUCE

Breast of veal isn't often cooked whole – it is most frequently sold minced or diced as pie veal – but it is delicious slow-cooked as a pot roast. A 1.5–2kg breast on the bone should be enough to feed four, but if your butcher only has smaller joints, you may need to buy a couple.

Serves 4

1 breast of veal, about 1.5–2kg
sea salt and freshly ground black pepper
3–4 tbsp cold-pressed rapeseed oil
100g butter, in pieces
1 tbsp fennel seeds, lightly pounded with a pestle and mortar or chopped
a handful of rosemary leaves
10–12 garlic cloves, peeled and roughly chopped

For the sauce

a couple of generous knobs of butter
3 medium onions, peeled and finely chopped
½ tbsp rosemary leaves
200ml double cream

Preheat the oven to 180°C/gas mark 4. Season the veal breast with salt and pepper. Heat a little of the rapeseed oil in a frying pan and brown the veal breast on both sides over a high heat. Transfer to a roasting tray, spoon over the rest of the oil and dot with the butter. Sprinkle the fennel, rosemary and garlic over the meat. Cover with foil and cook in the oven for an hour.

Remove the foil, baste the veal joint with the pan juices and continue cooking, uncovered, for another hour or until the veal is very tender, basting from time to time.

Meanwhile, to make the sauce, melt the butter in a pan and add the onions. Cover and cook very gently without colouring over a low heat for 5–6 minutes, stirring every so often, until they are very soft. Add the rosemary and cream, season and simmer until the liquor has reduced by about half. Ladle out a third of the sauce into a blender and purée until smooth, then return to the pan. Re-season if necessary and keep warm.

Either serve the veal as a whole joint and carve it at the table, serving the sauce separately, or carve it in the kitchen and serve on warmed plates with the sauce poured over.

BRAISED OXTAIL WITH SUMMER VEGETABLES

Oxtail has such a unique flavour that it's a shame to have it only as a winter dish. Here I'm serving it with summer peas, beans and carrots to make the point, but you can change the vegetables to suit the seasons.

Serves 4

1.5kg oxtail, cut into 2–3cm thick pieces and trimmed of excess fat

salt and freshly ground black pepper

50g plain flour, plus extra for dusting

a little vegetable oil, for oiling

60g butter, plus an extra generous knob

1 onion, peeled and finely chopped

2 garlic cloves, peeled and crushed

1 tsp thyme leaves

2 tsp tomato purée

100ml red wine

2 litres beef stock

250g small carrots, such as Chantenay, trimmed

60g podded peas

90–100g podded broad beans

½ tbsp chopped parsley

Preheat the oven to 220°C/gas mark 7. Season the oxtail pieces and dust lightly with flour. Place in a lightly oiled roasting tray and roast for 30 minutes, turning them halfway through to make sure they colour nicely on both sides. If cooking the braise in the oven, lower the setting to 160°C/gas mark 3.

Meanwhile, heat the 60g butter in a pressure cooker or a large ovenproof pan. Add the onion, garlic and thyme and cook gently for 3–4 minutes until soft, stirring every so often. Add the flour and tomato purée and stir well. Slowly add the red wine and beef stock, stirring to avoid lumps forming, then bring to the boil. Add the pieces of oxtail and turn to coat in the liquor. Now close and secure the pressure cooker lid, or cover the ovenproof pan with a tight-fitting lid.

Cook on the lowest possible heat (a heat-diffuser mat or simmer plate is useful), or in the oven if you're not using a pressure cooker. Check the oxtail after about 1 hour if using a pressure cooker, otherwise after 2 hours. It should be tender and easily removed from the bone; if not, replace the lid and cook for another 15 minutes or so under pressure, or up to another hour in the oven or over a low heat.

Skim off the fat from the sauce. If the sauce is not thick enough, strain it into another pan and simmer briskly until reduced and thickened, skimming every so often, then pour back over the meat.

Shortly before serving, cook the carrots, peas and broad beans separately in boiling salted water until tender. Remove the tough skins from larger beans.

To serve, melt the knob of butter in a pan, add the carrots, peas and broad beans and toss over a low heat to glaze, then season with salt and pepper and add the chopped parsley.

Divide the oxtail between warmed plates, spoon over the sauce and serve with the glazed vegetables.

CROSS-CUT RIBS BAKED IN A BARBECUE SAUCE

This recipe, using my favourite cross-cut ribs, leans more towards American barbecue cooking, although it is prepared with British ingredients. Serve the ribs with a simple salad or perhaps the Blue Monday salad (on page 60).

Deep-fried green tomatoes also make a great accompaniment, should you happen to have some unripe tomatoes in the garden. Coat chunky green tomato slices, about 1cm thick, in a cider-flavoured batter, deep-fry until golden and sprinkle with sea salt.

Serves 4

12–16 cross-cut beef ribs (see page 112)
1–2 tbsp vegetable oil

For the barbecue sauce
a couple of generous knobs of butter
4 large shallots, peeled and finely chopped
4 garlic cloves, peeled and crushed
200ml cider
200ml beef stock
60–80g tomato ketchup
60–80g HP sauce or Oxford sauce
½ tbsp Tewkesbury mustard
1 tbsp clear honey
1 small chilli, finely chopped
4 tbsp tomato purée
40ml Henderson's relish or Worcestershire sauce
salt and freshly ground black pepper

Preheat the oven to 150°C/gas mark 2. For the barbecue sauce, simply mix all the ingredients together in a bowl, seasoning with salt and pepper to taste.

Heat 1 tbsp oil in a large, heavy-based frying pan over a medium-high heat. When hot, fry the ribs in batches for 2–3 minutes on each side until they are nicely coloured, adding more oil to the pan as necessary. Once browned, transfer the ribs to a large ovenproof dish.

Pour the barbecue sauce over the ribs and toss to coat all over. Cook in the oven for about an hour or until the ribs are tender and glazed, and the meat is just falling away from the bone.

BEEF AND OYSTER PIE

Pies are a great way to use the less expensive, yet full-flavoured meat cuts, such as flank and shin of beef, mutton shoulder and neck, and ox cheeks. Tucking in a few shucked oysters adds a touch of luxury.

Serves 4

1kg trimmed flank or shin of beef
3 tbsp plain flour
salt and freshly ground black pepper
vegetable oil for frying
30g butter
1 medium onion, peeled and finely chopped
1 garlic clove, peeled and crushed
1 tsp tomato purée
200ml dark ale, such as Hix Oyster Ale or Guinness
1.5 litres hot beef stock
1 tsp chopped thyme leaves
1 small bay leaf
1–2 tsp cornflour (if needed)
12 large oysters, 8 shucked, 4 left in the half-shell

For the pastry
225g self-raising flour, plus extra for dusting
1 tsp salt
85g shredded beef suet
60g butter, chilled and coarsely grated
1 free-range medium egg, beaten, to glaze

For the parsley crust
a generous knob of butter
2 tbsp fresh white breadcrumbs
1 tbsp chopped parsley

Cut the meat roughly into 3cm cubes. Season half of the flour with salt and pepper and use to lightly flour the meat. Heat a little oil in a large, heavy-based frying pan and fry the meat in 2 or 3 batches over a high heat until nicely browned. Set aside on a plate.

Melt the butter in a large, heavy-based pan or flameproof casserole and fry the onion and garlic for a few minutes until lightly coloured. Add the remaining flour and tomato purée. Stir over a low heat for a minute or so, then slowly add the ale and hot stock, stirring to avoid lumps forming.

Add the beef with the thyme and bay leaf. Bring back to a simmer, cover and simmer very gently (ideally using a heat-diffuser mat or a simmer plate) for about 2 hours until the meat is tender. When the meat is cooked, the sauce should have thickened to a gravy-like consistency. If not, mix a little cornflour to a paste with 1 tbsp water, stir into the sauce and simmer, stirring, for a few minutes. Leave to cool.

To make the pastry, mix the flour, salt, suet and butter together in a large bowl and make a well in the centre. Mix in enough water (about 150ml) to form a smooth dough and knead for a minute.

Spoon the cooled filling into 4 individual pie dishes (or a large dish) to about 1cm from the rim. Roll the pastry out on a floured surface to a 7–8 mm thickness. Cut out 4 discs to make pie lids (or one large lid for a big pie), about 2cm larger all round than the pie dish(es). Brush the edges of the pastry with a little of the beaten egg.

Lay the pastry over the filling, pressing the egg-washed sides onto the rim of the dish(es). Cut a 2cm hole in the centre but leave the pastry circle in position. Let rest in a cool place for 30 minutes.

Preheat the oven to 200°C/gas mark 6. Brush the pie(s) with beaten egg and bake for 30–35 minutes (or 40–50 minutes for a large one) until the pastry is golden. Meanwhile, for the parsley crust, melt the butter in a pan, mix in the breadcrumbs and parsley, and season with salt and pepper.

Once the pie(s) are ready, remove the pastry disc(s) in the centre and pop in the shucked oysters. Return to the oven for 10 minutes. In the meantime, heat the grill. Scatter the parsley crust over the oysters in their half-shell and grill until golden. Place over the hole in the pie and serve.

SIDES

I view side orders as a crucial part of a restaurant menu. A good selection of seasonal vegetables, including a few different potato dishes, helps keep the menu interesting and allows customers to choose what they fancy. Of course it's important that the sides on the menu are suitable accompaniments for the main dishes on offer.

Some restaurants don't offer a choice of side dishes on the menu at all; instead serving up a random assortment of vegetables that are not always appropriate to the main dish ordered. This doesn't make any sense to me.

A few of the main courses on the Oyster & Chop House menu, such as braises and hotpots, are complete in themselves because vegetables are an integral part. Here sides become superfluous, unless a customer chooses to order a side salad or an extra vegetable.

As with the rest of the menu, seasonality is always a prime consideration. A customer should be able to look at the side order menu and tell exactly what time of the year it is by the dishes on offer.

FRIED SQUASH OR COURGETTE FLOWERS

Courgettes and other members of the squash family produce great flowers that can be harvested continually for 2 or 3 months during the summer and cooked as a snack, starter or accompaniment. The flowers are best harvested when the sun is out and when they have fully opened. I like them simply fried in a light batter until crisp. On menus you often see stuffed courgette flowers, but the filling adds moisture, which tends to make the batter go soggy.

Serves 4

8 large courgette, squash or pumpkin flowers, with their stalks
120g self-raising flour, plus extra for dusting
20–30g mature Cheddar cheese, finely grated
salt and freshly ground black pepper
vegetable or corn oil for deep-frying

Check that the flowers are clean and free from insects. To make the batter, place the flour in a bowl and slowly whisk in 200ml ice-cold water to form a thickish batter. Add the grated cheese, season with salt and pepper and give it a final whisk.

Heat an 8cm depth of oil in a deep-fat fryer or other suitable deep, heavy pan to 160–180°C, or until a little batter dropped into the oil turns golden brown after a minute or so.

Have a shallow bowl of flour ready. One at a time, dip the flowers into the flour, shaking off any excess, then dip into the batter to coat and drop into the hot oil. Deep-fry 3 or 4 flowers at a time, moving them around in the oil with a spoon, for a couple of minutes until they are crisp and light golden.

Remove the courgette flowers with a slotted spoon and put on a plate lined with kitchen paper to drain. Season lightly with salt and serve.

AUTUMN GREENS WITH WILD MUSHROOMS

Cabbage and greens often benefit from being spruced up with another ingredient. A singular or a mix of wild mushrooms does the trick.

Serves 4

1 head of green cabbage, or a mixture of greens
salt and freshly ground black pepper
100g butter
1 small onion, peeled and finely chopped
2 garlic cloves, peeled and crushed
120–150g wild mushrooms, cleaned

Cut the cabbage or greens roughly into 2–3cm chunks and wash well. Add to a pan of boiling salted water, bring back to the boil and cook for 3–5 minutes until just tender. Drain thoroughly in a colander.

Meanwhile, melt half of the butter in a frying pan and gently cook the onion and garlic for 3–4 minutes to soften.

Add the rest of the butter to the pan. Once melted, add the mushrooms and cook over a medium heat for 4–5 minutes until tender, turning frequently and seasoning after a couple of minutes.

Add the cabbage to the mushrooms and toss them together over the heat until hot. Check the seasoning and serve at once.

SCRUMPY BATTERED ONIONS

This is the kind of dish you can eat as a bar snack, order at the table to nibble on as a starter, or have as a comforting side dish. At The Oyster & Chop House our fried onions go down a treat with some of those hefty cuts of meat. You can use a single type of onion or a selection, as I have here.

Serves 4

1 medium yellow onion, peeled
4 spring onions, trimmed
1 medium red onion, peeled
80g self-raising flour
about 100–120ml scrumpy or cider to mix
salt and freshly ground black pepper
vegetable or corn oil for deep-frying
plain flour for dusting
onion salt to serve

Cut the yellow onion into 5mm thick rings; cut each spring onion into 4 lengths; halve the red onion and cut into 5mm thick half-moon slices. Separate the slices and rings.

To make the batter, put the flour into a bowl and whisk in enough of the cider to make a smooth, thick batter. Season with salt and pepper. Leave to rest for about 30 minutes.

Heat an 8cm depth of oil in a deep-fat fryer or other suitable deep, heavy pan to 160–180°C. Season the flour for dusting well.

To test that the batter is the correct thickness, dust a piece of onion in flour, then coat in batter and immerse in the hot oil. The batter should adhere and the onion should cook up crisp; if not, adjust the batter with more cider or flour.

You'll need to cook the onions in 2 or 3 batches. Toss the first batch in the flour, shaking off excess, then dip into the batter to coat and drop into the hot oil. Deep-fry for about 3–4 minutes until nicely coloured, turning them occasionally with a slotted spoon. Drain on kitchen paper, then scatter with onion salt. Eat straight away or keep hot while you cook the rest, then serve at once.

CAULIFLOWER CHEESE

We have two growing seasons for cauliflower in the UK: in the West Country it is a winter crop, while in the North of England it's a summer harvest. Both are excellent and there are many different ways you can treat this vegetable. Cauliflower cheese is a firm favourite, but you can also roast it, or deep-fry it in batter, or serve it as a purée which is particularly good with fish or offal.

Serves 4

1 medium cauliflower
500ml milk
salt and freshly ground black pepper
50g butter
50g plain flour
1 small bay leaf
200ml double cream
100g mature Cheddar cheese, grated
1 large egg yolk

Preheat the oven to 200°C/gas mark 6. Cut the cauliflower into large florets. Pour the milk into a saucepan, season and bring to the boil. Add the cauliflower florets and cook for 7–8 minutes or until just tender. Drain in a colander over a bowl, reserving the milk.

Melt the butter in a heavy-based saucepan, then stir in the flour and cook, stirring, over a low heat for 30 seconds. Gradually whisk in the milk, keeping the mixture smooth. Add the bay leaf, re-season and simmer very gently for about 15 minutes, stirring from time to time.

Add the cream and simmer for a further 5 minutes: the sauce should be quite thick by now; if not simmer gently until it is a thick coating consistency. Remove the bay leaf, then stir in three-quarters of the grated cheese and the egg yolk.

Mix the cauliflower with the sauce and transfer to an ovenproof serving dish. Scatter the rest of the cheese over the surface and bake in the oven for about 15 minutes or until nicely browned.

RUNNER BEAN PURÉE

You may think it's a bit extravagant to purée runner beans but it is a great way to serve them if you have a glut in your garden, or if you just fancy a change. Try serving this side with grilled meat or deep-fried fish, or top a smaller portion with grilled scallops and scatter some blanched shredded runner beans over them for a lovely summery starter.

Serves 4–6

500g runner beans, trimmed
salt and freshly ground black pepper
a few knobs of butter

Roughly chop the runner beans. Bring a pan of salted water to the boil, drop in the beans and cook for 5–7 minutes until just tender, then drain.

Tip the beans into a blender or food processor and blend to a purée – as coarse or smooth as you like; you may need to add a little water.

Return the purée to the pan and place over a low heat. Add the butter, season with salt and pepper to taste, then serve.

MINTED PEAS WITH THEIR SHOOTS

Peas are an all-time great summer vegetable that can involve the whole family – whether it's harvesting from the garden or a day out at a pick-your-own farm. Pea shoots or tendrils are often overlooked, yet I love using them in salads or just quickly tossing them in butter to eat on their own or with the peas themselves.

Serves 4–6

300–400g freshly podded peas (about 1kg before podding)
salt and freshly ground black pepper
1½ tsp caster sugar
a handful of mint sprigs, leaves stripped, stalks reserved
60g butter
a couple of handfuls of pea shoots

For the peas, bring a pan of salted water to the boil with the sugar and mint stalks added. Tip in the peas and simmer for 4–5 minutes or until tender, then drain and discard the mint stalks.

Melt the butter in a wide pan. Add the pea shoots, quickly season with salt and pepper and toss for a few seconds until they are just wilted.

Tip in the cooked peas, toss to combine and re-season if necessary before serving.

CREAMED SPINACH

Creamed spinach makes a delicious comforting accompaniment to simply grilled meat or fish. It has a feeling of luxuriousness about it the moment you put it into your mouth. Cooked in this way it almost acts like a sauce for grilled meat or fish.

Serves 4–6

750–800g spinach, thick stalks removed and washed
salt and freshly ground black pepper
200ml double cream

Bring a pan of salted water to the boil. Plunge in the spinach leaves and cook for 2–3 minutes until tender. Drain in a colander, refresh under the cold tap and squeeze out any excess water.

Tip the spinach into a food processor and blend as smoothly or as coarsely as you wish. You can take it to this stage in advance if you like, then finish at the last minute.

Simmer the cream in a saucepan until reduced by about half, then stir in the spinach and season with salt and pepper to taste. Cook over a low heat for a minute or so, stirring every so often, until the spinach is hot. Serve immediately.

SPROUTING BROCCOLI WITH HERBS AND HAZELNUTS

A herby, nutty breadcrumb crust gives a nice contrast to sprouting broccoli and it works well with other vegetables too, especially cauliflower, marrow and squash.

Serves 4

350–400g tender sprouting broccoli

For the crust
40–50g fresh white breadcrumbs
50g hazelnuts, chopped
1 tbsp cold-pressed rapeseed oil
a couple of generous knobs of butter
4 shallots, peeled and finely chopped
2 garlic cloves, peeled and crushed
2–3 tbsp finely chopped mixed herbs, such as parsley, chervil, tarragon and chives
salt and freshly ground black pepper

For the crust, preheat the grill to medium. In a bowl, toss the breadcrumbs and chopped hazelnuts together with the rapeseed oil and scatter on a baking tray. Toast under the grill for 3–5 minutes until golden, turning once or twice to ensure the mixture colours evenly.

Meanwhile, melt the butter in a pan and gently cook the shallots and garlic for a few minutes until softened. Stir in the breadcrumbs and herbs until well mixed and season with salt and pepper.

When ready to serve, cook the broccoli in boiling salted water for about 4–5 minutes, so that it is still just a little firm to the bite. Drain thoroughly and transfer to a warmed serving dish. Scatter the breadcrumb mixture over the top and serve.

BAKED PARSNIPS WITH LANCASHIRE CHEESE

This is an excellent alternative to a traditional gratin dauphinois that could also be made with turnip, squash or even swede. It's a great sharing dish to put in the middle of the table for guests to help themselves.

Serves 4–6

750g parsnips, peeled
400ml double cream
400ml milk
a good pinch of freshly grated nutmeg
2 garlic cloves, peeled and crushed
salt and freshly ground black pepper
150g Lancashire cheese, grated
2 tbsp fresh white breadcrumbs
1 tbsp chopped parsley

Preheat the oven to 160°C/gas mark 3. Cut the parsnips into rough 2–3cm chunks.

Pour the cream and milk into a saucepan, add the nutmeg and garlic, and season generously with salt and pepper. Bring to the boil, then turn off the heat and leave to cool slightly.

Put the parsnips into a shallow ovenproof (gratin-type) dish and mix with all but 1 tbsp of the cheese. Pour the cream mixture over the top.

Stand the dish in a roasting tray and pour in enough boiling water to come halfway up the side of the dish (to create a bain-marie). Cook in the oven for about an hour until the parsnips are cooked through.

Preheat the grill to medium. Mix the breadcrumbs with the chopped parsley and remaining 1 tbsp grated cheese. Scatter over the parsnip bake and place under the grill for a few minutes until golden. Serve at once, or cover with foil and leave in a low oven until ready to serve.

STRAW POTATOES

Conveniently, these fine chips can be prepared ahead and fried for the second time just before serving. In between blanching and re-frying place on a tray, cover and refrigerate until required.

You can serve the chips with just about anything, from grilled and roasted meat, poultry and game to fish and shellfish – especially mussels.

Serves 4

4 large chipping potatoes, such as Yukon Gold, Spunta or Maris Piper, peeled
vegetable or corn oil for deep-frying
10 garlic cloves, peeled and thinly sliced
sea salt

Using a mandolin with a shredding attachment or a sharp knife, cut the potatoes into long matchsticks, about 3mm thick. Wash them well in a couple of changes of cold water to remove excess starch, then drain and pat dry on a clean tea towel.

Heat an 8cm depth of oil in a deep-fat fryer or other suitable deep, heavy pan to 120–140°C. Blanch the matchstick potatoes in manageable batches (a couple of handfuls at a time) for 2–3 minutes, then remove with a slotted spoon and drain in a colander.

Increase the temperature of the oil to 160–180°C and re-fry the potatoes with the garlic slices in batches, moving them around in the pan, until golden and crisp. Remove with a slotted spoon and drain on kitchen paper. Sprinkle with sea salt and serve immediately.

Alternatively, you can keep the straw potatoes warm, uncovered, on a baking tray in a low oven until ready to serve. They should stay crisp but if not you can briefly re-fry them in hot oil to crisp them up again.

DESSERTS

I tend to keep our dessert menu short and sweet, basing it largely around old-fashioned nursery puddings and other classic favourites, such as crumbles, tarts and jellies. I'm always looking to make the most of our homegrown fruits, however short their season, and the dessert menu reflects this. Berries, cherries and currants feature in the summer; pears, plums and apples through autumn and winter; and outdoor rhubarb from early spring.

We have fun with jellies all the year round, suspending berries in elderflower and Perry jelly in the summer, and making them a bit more alcoholic in the winter with sloe gin, absinth and Somerset eau-de-vie, using the liquor from our Hix fix cherries.

The dessert menu is also an opportunity to feature some of our artisan producers including Willie Harcourt Couze, eccentric Devon chocolate producer, and Julian Temperley, Somerset's unconventional cider maker. They come together in my truffle recipe (on page 185) and Julian's oak-aged cider brandy inspired my Shipwreck tart (on page 181).

You'll find the desserts here easy to replicate at home – and easy to adapt with the seasons. Enjoy...

ELDERFLOWER AND BUTTERMILK PUDDING WITH SUMMER FRUITS

This smooth, creamy pudding is rather like an Italian panna cotta. We don't use buttermilk that much in cooking, although in Ireland it's a fairly commonplace ingredient. You can get hold of it in good supermarkets and dairy shops; otherwise just use Jersey milk.

You can introduce different fruits here as they come into season; in winter a compote of dried fruits or preserved fruits in alcohol works well.

Serves 4

12g leaf gelatine (4 sheets)
350ml buttermilk
50g caster sugar
250ml double cream
100ml good-quality elderflower cordial

For the summer fruits
100g strawberries, hulled
30g caster sugar
50g raspberries
50g blueberries
50g redcurrants

Soak the leaf gelatine in a bowl of cold water for a few minutes to soften. Meanwhile, pour 100ml of the buttermilk into a saucepan, add the sugar and bring to the boil over a medium-low heat, stirring occasionally to encourage the sugar to dissolve.

Squeeze the gelatine leaves to remove excess water. Remove the buttermilk from the heat, add the gelatine and stir until dissolved. Leave to cool until barely warm.

Whisk the cream, elderflower cordial and the rest of the buttermilk into the mixture. Pour into dariole moulds, ramekins or coffee cups and place in the fridge for 2–3 hours or overnight to set.

In the meantime, put the strawberries and 30g sugar into a saucepan over a low heat and simmer very gently for about 5 minutes until the berries have turned to a mush. Strain through a fine-meshed sieve into a bowl, pushing down on the pulp with the back of a spoon to extract as much juice as possible. Leave to cool.

To serve, briefly dip the pudding moulds in hot water, then invert onto serving plates and shake gently to turn out. Scatter the raspberries, blueberries and redcurrants around the puddings and spoon the strawberry sauce over them.

SLOE GIN JELLY SHOTS

If you make your own sloe gin then this is a fun way to show it off at a party and it's a great talking point. Otherwise, it's not difficult to find good-quality sloe gin in the shops. Depending on how strong you want your jellies to be, you can up the gin and use less water.

Makes 16–20

1 tbsp caster sugar
6g leaf gelatine (2 sheets)
400ml sloe gin
thick Jersey cream (optional) to serve

Bring 200ml water to the boil in a saucepan, add the sugar and stir until dissolved, then remove from the heat.

Soak the gelatine leaves in a shallow bowl of cold water for a minute or so until soft. Squeeze out the excess water, then add to the sugar syrup and stir until melted. Stir in the sloe gin.

Pour into shot glasses and place in the fridge for a couple of hours or so until the jelly is set. Serve topped with a spoonful of thick cream if you like.

CHOCOLATE MOUSSE

Of all the chocolate mousse recipes that I've used over the years, this one is the simplest and yields the best results by far. It's wonderfully indulgent and comforting.

Serves 4–6

250g good-quality dark chocolate, about 70% cocoa solids, broken into small pieces
50g unsalted butter, softened
6 very fresh free-range medium eggs, separated, plus 3 extra egg whites
40g caster sugar
chocolate curls (shaved from a block of chocolate with a peeler) to finish

Melt the chocolate in a heatproof bowl over a pan of simmering water, stirring every so often and making sure the bowl isn't touching the water. Remove from the heat and beat in the butter, using a whisk or spoon, until smooth. Beat the egg yolks in another bowl and set aside.

In a clean, grease-free bowl, whisk the egg whites until frothy but not stiff, using a mixer or an electric whisk on a medium-high speed. Add half the sugar and continue whisking on a low setting until stiff. Add the rest of the sugar and whisk until the egg whites stiffen up further. Now fold in the beaten egg yolks using a metal spoon.

Carefully stir half of this into the chocolate mixture, using a whisk, then fold in the rest with a large spoon until evenly combined. Pour into a large serving dish and leave to set for a couple of hours, or overnight.

To serve, scoop a portion of mousse onto each serving plate and finish with chocolate curls.

PEARS IN PERRY

Poaching pears in their own alcohol, Perry, makes sense – I'm not sure why I didn't think of it before Matthew Fort gave me the idea. You can serve the pears with clotted cream or ice cream, or with blackberries and blackberry rippled cream as I have here.

Serves 4

4 firm pears
500ml Perry
4 cloves
a small piece of cinnamon stick
6 black peppercorns
2 tbsp caster sugar
a couple of handfuls of blackberries (optional)
clotted cream or ice cream to serve

Peel the pears, leaving the stalks intact, and cut a thin sliver off the base of each one so they will stand upright.

Put the Perry, cloves, cinnamon, peppercorns and caster sugar into a heavy-based saucepan and add the pears. Lay a piece of greaseproof paper over the fruit. Bring to a simmer and poach gently for about 45 minutes until the pears are soft and tender but still holding their shape.

Lift out the poached pears, using a slotted spoon, and set aside on a plate.

Continue to simmer the liquor in the pan until it has reduced by about two-thirds and thickened. Return the pears to the liquor and leave to cool.

To serve, stand each pear in a deep serving plate and spoon over some of the reduced liquor. Add a few blackberries, if using, and a scoop of clotted cream or ice cream.

RHUBARB CRUMBLE AND CUSTARD ICE CREAM

You can have a lot of fun with home-made ices. I love transforming classic British puddings into ice creams and this is one of my favourites. The rhubarb is simply folded into a basic vanilla ice cream and the crumble is churned through at the last minute. It is best eaten on the day it is made, or within a few days.

Serves 6–8

400ml creamy milk, such as gold top, Guernsey or Jersey

1½ vanilla pods or ½ tsp vanilla extract

6 free-range medium egg yolks

150g caster sugar

400ml Jersey or clotted cream, or a mixture

For the rhubarb

600g rhubarb, trimmed

200g caster sugar

1 tsp cornflour, mixed with 2 tbsp cold water

For the crumble topping

160g plain flour

80g cold butter, cut into small pieces

90g soft brown sugar

50g oats

60–80g shelled nuts, such as walnuts, hazelnuts and/or almonds, coarsely chopped

3 tbsp pumpkin seeds

Pour the milk into a saucepan. Split the vanilla pods lengthways, scrape out the seeds with a knife and add them to the milk with the empty pods. (If using vanilla extract, don't add it yet.) Slowly bring the milk to the boil, then take the pan off the heat and remove the empty vanilla pods.

Whisk the egg yolks and sugar together in a bowl, then pour on the hot milk, whisking as you do so. Return to the pan and cook gently over a low heat, stirring constantly with a wooden spoon, for about 5 minutes until the custard thickens; don't let it boil. Pour into a bowl and whisk in the cream. (Add the vanilla extract now, if using.) Cover the surface with a sheet of greaseproof paper to prevent a skin forming and leave to cool.

Preheat the oven to 190°C/gas mark 5. Cut the rhubarb roughly into 2cm pieces, place in an ovenproof dish and scatter with the sugar. Cover with foil and cook in the oven for about 30 minutes until tender. Pour the juice from the rhubarb into a saucepan and bring to a simmer. Stir the blended cornflour into the liquor and cook, stirring, for a minute or so to thicken, then stir back into the rhubarb. Leave to cool.

To make the crumble, put the flour into a bowl and rub in the butter until the mixture is the texture of breadcrumbs. Mix in the sugar, followed by the oats, nuts and pumpkin seeds. Scatter on a baking tray and bake for about 15 minutes until golden. Set aside to cool.

Churn the custard in an ice-cream machine until thickened and almost frozen to the right consistency for serving, then fold in the rhubarb and half of the crumble mixture. Transfer to a suitable container and place in the freezer until needed. Keep the rest of the crumble in an airtight container.

To serve, scoop the ice cream into glass bowls and scatter the reserved crumble on top.

JERSEY RICE PUDDING WITH RHUBARB

A good rice pudding relies on the use of quality ingredients and careful cooking. You can serve this with whatever fruits happen to be in season. A compote of plums and autumn berries, spiced with a little cinnamon, is delicious. Or you could simply top the pudding with a dollop of strawberry jam if you prefer.

Serves 6

1–1.5 litres Jersey milk
70–90g caster sugar, to taste
½ vanilla pod
100g good-quality short-grain pudding rice
500ml thick Jersey or double cream

For the rhubarb
300–400g rhubarb, trimmed and washed
120g caster sugar

Pour 1 litre milk into a heavy-based saucepan and add 70g of the sugar. Split the vanilla pod lengthways, scrape out the seeds with the tip of a knife and add them to the milk along with the empty pod. Bring the milk to the boil, stirring to dissolve the sugar, then add the rice.

Simmer very gently, stirring regularly, for about 45 minutes until the rice is soft. (Use a simmer plate or a heat-diffuser mat if you have one to maintain a steady low heat.) Add a little more milk during cooking if the rice pudding seems to be getting too thick. Taste for sweetness, stirring in a bit more sugar if you think it is needed.

Leave the pudding to stand for about half an hour, stirring from time to time. Now remove the vanilla pod and stir in two-thirds of the cream. Allow to cool, again stirring every so often.

For the rhubarb, preheat the oven to 200°C/gas mark 6. Cut the rhubarb roughly into 1cm pieces. Place in a baking tray or ovenproof dish and scatter over the caster sugar. Cover with foil and cook in the oven for about 30 minutes until the rhubarb is tender.

Carefully pour off the cooking juices from the rhubarb into a saucepan. Bring to the boil and let bubble until reduced by about half and thickened. Pour back over the rhubarb and leave to cool.

Before serving, stir the rest of the cream into the rice pudding. Serve at room temperature or warm, with the rhubarb spooned on top.

INDIVIDUAL BRAMBLE PIES

If you are a forager you're unlikely to miss out on making the most of our autumn abundance of blackberries – or brambles. You can add other fruits, such as blueberries or elderberries if you wish, or stick to the traditional blackberry and apple combination. You can also use frozen blackberries.

Serves 4

For the pastry
110g butter, softened, plus extra to grease
135g caster sugar
225g strong plain flour, plus extra for dusting
a pinch of salt
½ tsp baking powder
125ml double cream

For the filling
800g blackberries
120g caster sugar
1 tsp arrowroot or cornflour, mixed with 1 tbsp cold water

To finish
1 free-range medium egg white, mixed with 1 tbsp caster sugar
icing sugar for dusting

To serve
thick cream or crème fraîche

First make the pastry. In a food processor or electric mixer, or by hand, cream the butter and sugar together until smooth. Sift the flour, salt and baking powder together and stir into the creamed mixture until evenly combined. Now slowly incorporate the cream until well mixed.

Knead the dough lightly, then divide into 2 portions, one slightly bigger than the other. Shape each into a ball, wrap in cling film and refrigerate for 30 minutes.

Lightly butter four 10cm individual tart tins, about 3cm deep. Roll out the slightly larger ball of pastry on a lightly floured surface to about a 3mm thickness. Using an 18cm plate as a guide, cut out 4 discs. Use to line the tart tins, leaving about 5mm pastry overhanging the edge.

Roll out the other portion of pastry and cut 4 discs, a little more than 10cm in diameter, for the pie lids. Place on a tray. Put the lined tart tins and pastry discs in the fridge and leave to rest for 1 hour.

Meanwhile, to make the filling, put 200g of the blackberries into a saucepan with the sugar and 1 tbsp water. Bring to a simmer and cook gently for 3–4 minutes. Add the blended arrowroot and simmer for another 2–3 minutes, stirring occasionally. Strain through a fine-meshed sieve into a bowl and leave to cool a little, then mix in the rest of the blackberries.

Preheat the oven to 200°C/gas mark 6. Remove the pastry from the fridge. Using a slotted spoon, fill the pastry cases with the blackberry filling. Moisten with the juice from the fruit, but don't add too much. Brush the pastry rim with water, then lay the pastry lids over the pies, pressing the edges together to seal with your fingers.

Brush the tops with the egg white and sugar mix, then make a small slit in the centre with the point of a knife. Put the tart tins on a baking tray and bake in the oven for 20–25 minutes until golden, turning the oven down a little or covering loosely with foil if they appear to be colouring too quickly.

Leave the pies to rest for about 15 minutes, then unmould onto plates. Dust with icing sugar and serve with a generous spoonful of thick cream or crème fraîche.

APPLE BREAD PUDDING

Bread pudding is of one of those recipes that you can tweak and add other ingredients to very easily. Here I've included apples and cider to give it a real taste of the West Country. Serve warm with thick cream or ice cream, or custard of you prefer.

Serves 6–8

500ml medium cider
200g caster sugar, plus extra for dusting
½ tsp ground cinnamon
½ tsp ground mixed spice
60g sultanas
60g raisins
grated zest of ½ orange
500g brown or white bread, crusts removed
4 medium crisp dessert apples, such as Cox's
50g butter
4 free-range medium eggs, beaten
thick Jersey cream or ice cream to serve

Put the cider, sugar, spices, sultanas, raisins and orange zest into a saucepan and bring to the boil. Meanwhile, break the bread into small pieces and place in a bowl. Tip the cider mixture over the bread and stir to mix. Cover the bowl with cling film and leave to stand overnight.

The next day, peel, quarter, core and slice the apples. Melt the butter in a large frying pan and fry the apples over a medium heat, stirring occasionally, for 3–4 minutes until lightly coloured. Set aside to cool.

Preheat the oven to 180°C/gas mark 4. Line the base and sides of a 20cm square baking tin, about 6cm deep, with greaseproof paper.

Fold the beaten eggs into the bread mixture, then fold in the cooled apples. Spoon the mixture into the prepared tin and bake for about 30–40 minutes until firm. Dust the top with caster sugar while still hot. Serve with cream or ice cream.

ROAST PLUMS WITH COBNUTS AND CLOTTED CREAM

We have lots of varieties of plums in the UK, from large Victorias to small greengages. You can use any variety for this dish, or a mixture. Cobnut trees are pretty specific to Kent; if you are unable to get hold of any cobnuts, use hazelnuts instead.

Serves 4

12–18 Victoria or other plums, depending on size
6 tbsp caster sugar

For the topping
2 tbsp plain flour
40g hard butter, chopped into small pieces
½ tbsp brown sugar
4 tbsp oats
24–30 cobnuts, shelled and roughly chopped

To serve
clotted cream or thick Jersey cream

Preheat the oven to 200°C/gas mark 6. First make the topping: put the flour and butter into a bowl and rub together with your fingers to a breadcrumb-like consistency. Stir in the brown sugar, then mix in the oats and cobnuts. Spread out on a baking tray.

Halve the plums, place cut-side up on another baking tray and sprinkle with the caster sugar.

Place both of the trays in the oven and bake for 15–20 minutes until the plums are lightly coloured and softened and the topping is golden; you may need to take the topping out before the plums.

Leave the plums to cool slightly, then transfer them to individual serving bowls and spoon over the cooking juices. Scatter over the cobnut topping and top with a generous dollop of cream.

STRAWBERRY AND SPARKLING WINE JELLY

I confess to being a bit of a jelly freak. There is no end to what you can make and do with jellies whatever the time of the year. This is a pretty posh jelly and not that cheap to make, but if you're going to the trouble of picking or buying wild or homegrown strawberries, then it's worth splashing out on Champagne or, better still, Nyetimber – the best sparkling wine produced in the UK (see page 34).

Of course you can adapt the recipe, using Perry or cider instead of sparkling wine, and a mixture of berries, such as raspberries, blueberries and small strawberries. For a non-alcoholic jelly, use elderflower cordial, diluted with water or apple juice.

Serves 4

12g leaf gelatine (4 sheets)

700ml fine-quality sparkling wine, such as Nyetimber or Chapel Down, or Champagne

50g caster sugar

120g strawberries, hulled

thick Jersey cream, to serve

Soak the leaf gelatine in a bowl of cold water for a few minutes to soften. Meanwhile, pour 200ml of the sparkling wine into a saucepan, add the sugar and bring to the boil over a medium-low heat, stirring occasionally to encourage the sugar to dissolve. Take off the heat.

Squeeze the gelatine leaves to remove excess water, then add to the wine syrup and stir until fully dissolved. Now stir in the rest of the sparkling wine. Leave to cool until barely warm, but don't allow the jelly to set.

Divide half of the strawberries between individual jelly moulds or attractive Martini glasses, then carefully pour in half of the cooled jelly, ensuring the berries are evenly distributed. Place in the fridge for an hour or so until set. Keep the rest of the jelly at room temperature, making sure it does not set.

Once the jellies have set, arrange the rest of the strawberries on top and pour on the rest of the jelly. (Setting the jelly in two stages allows the berries to stay suspended in the jelly so they don't float to the surface.) Return the jellies to the fridge to set.

To serve, briefly dip the pudding moulds, if using, in hot water, then invert onto serving plates and shake gently to turn out. Or set the Martini glasses on plates. Serve with thick Jersey cream.

SHIPWRECK TART

This tart was inspired by Julian Temperley's 10-year-old Shipwreck Somerset cider brandy, which is aged in oak barrels washed up on Branscome beach in Devon from the shipwrecked Napoli, hence the title.

Serves 8–10

For the pastry

225g unsalted butter, softened, plus extra for greasing

2 free-range medium egg yolks

1 tablespoon caster sugar

275g plain flour, plus extra for dusting

For the filling

3 free-range medium eggs, beaten

200g soft brown sugar

220g golden syrup

120ml cider brandy (ideally Shipwreck, see above)

100g unsalted butter, melted

1 tsp vanilla extract

100g walnuts, roughly chopped

100g hazelnuts, roughly chopped

100g shelled roasted chestnuts, roughly chopped

a pinch of salt

To serve

vanilla ice cream, crème fraîche or double cream

To make the pastry, in a food processor or electric mixer, or by hand, beat the butter and egg yolks together until smooth, then beat in the sugar. Mix in the flour until evenly combined, but don't overwork. Knead the dough lightly and shape into a ball. Wrap in cling film and refrigerate for 30 minutes.

Butter a 25cm loose-based tart tin. Roll out the pastry on a floured surface to a large circle, 3–4mm thick, and use to line the tin. Trim the edges and refrigerate for 1 hour.

Preheat the oven to 180°C/gas mark 4. To make the filling, blitz all the ingredients, except the nuts, in a food processor until smooth. Transfer to a bowl and fold in the nuts until evenly combined.

Fill the tart case with the nut mixture and bake for 20–25 minutes until golden brown. Serve with vanilla ice cream, crème fraîche or double cream.

CORNISH SAFFRON CUSTARD TARTS

This is a nod to past Cornish saffron growing. Some traditional Cornish cakes are still made with saffron, but these days it is imported, mostly from Iran and Spain.

Makes 10–12 mini tarts

250–300g ready-made all-butter puff pastry

plain flour for dusting

300ml single cream

a good pinch of saffron strands

4 free-range medium egg yolks

50g caster sugar

1½ tsp cornflour

Roll out the pastry on a lightly floured surface to a 3mm thickness and prick it thoroughly all over with a fork. Loosely fold into three, wrap in cling film and leave to rest in the fridge for 30–40 minutes.

Have ready a 12-hole muffin tray. Unfold the pastry and cut out circles, using a 9–10cm cutter. Use to line the muffin tins, pushing the pastry into the corners and trimming the tops with a sharp knife. Line with discs of greaseproof paper and baking beans and rest in the fridge for 15 minutes.

Preheat the oven to 180°C/gas mark 4. Bake the tart cases for 10–15 minutes until they begin to colour, then remove the paper and beans and leave to cool for a few minutes.

Meanwhile, put the cream and saffron into a small saucepan and bring to the boil. Take off the heat and leave to infuse for 10 minutes.

In a bowl, mix together the egg yolks, sugar and cornflour. Pour the infused cream onto the egg mixture, stirring well with a whisk. Return to the pan and cook over a low heat for several minutes, stirring constantly with a wooden spoon until the custard thickens; don't let it boil. Pour into a jug.

Pour the saffron custard into the tart cases and bake for 10–12 minutes until set. Leave to cool a little, then loosen the tarts with a small knife and carefully remove from the tin. Serve warm or cold.

WHITE PORT AND STRAWBERRY TRIFLE

This luxurious trifle was inspired by a trip to Portugal to visit one of our wine suppliers, Quinta de La Rosa, who also produces fine white port. I'm not sure why sherry is traditionally used in a trifle, perhaps it's to use up what's left after Christmas, but having enjoyed white port as an apéritif in Portugal, I thought I'd give it a go instead. It worked a treat.

Serves 4

For the jelly
100–120g strawberries, hulled and chopped
100g caster sugar
6g leaf gelatine (2 sheets)
200ml white port

For the base
50g sponge cake
100ml white port
150g strawberries, hulled and sliced

For the custard
300ml double cream
½ vanilla pod
5 free-range medium egg yolks
60g caster sugar
2 tsp cornflour

For the topping
250ml double cream
50–60g strawberries, hulled and sliced
20–30g flaked almonds, lightly toasted, or crushed macaroons

For the jelly, put the chopped strawberries, 200ml water and the sugar into a saucepan. Bring to the boil, then lower the heat and simmer gently for a couple of minutes.

Meanwhile, soak the gelatine leaves in cold water to cover for a few minutes to soften. Take off the heat. Squeeze the gelatine to remove excess water, add to the strawberry mixture and stir until dissolved. Strain the mixture through a fine sieve into a bowl and leave to cool a little, then add the white port.

For the trifle base, break the sponge into pieces and arrange in a layer in the bottom of a glass serving bowl or 4 individual dishes. Sprinkle the port evenly over the sponge and lay the strawberries on top. Pour over the cooled (but not set) jelly so it just covers the strawberries and put in the fridge for an hour or so to set.

Meanwhile, make the custard. Pour the cream into a heavy-based saucepan. Split the vanilla pod lengthways, scrape out the seeds with a knife and add them to the cream with the empty pod. Slowly bring to the boil, then remove from the heat and leave to infuse for about 10 minutes.

In a bowl, mix the egg yolks, sugar and cornflour together. Take out the vanilla pod and pour the cream onto the egg mix, whisking well. Return to the pan and cook gently over a low heat, stirring constantly with a wooden spoon until the custard thickens; don't let it boil. Pour into a bowl, cover the surface with a sheet of greaseproof paper to prevent a skin forming and leave to cool.

Once the jelly has set, spoon the cooled custard on top. Cover and refrigerate for half an hour or so until the custard has set.

For the topping, softly whip the cream, then spoon on top of the trifle. Decorate with the strawberry slices and toasted almonds or crushed macaroons.

VENEZUELAN BLACK AND CIDER BRANDY TRUFFLES

Time to celebrate two excellent West Country artisan products together in a truffle: Willie Harcourt Couze's 100% cacao black chocolate, made from selected Venezuelan cacao pods in Devon, and Julian Temperley's Somerset cider brandy.

Makes about 30

650g good-quality dark chocolate, finely chopped
400ml double cream
50g Venezuelan black chocolate
200g unsalted butter, softened
100ml Somerset cider brandy
60g good-quality cocoa powder

Set aside 250g of the dark chocolate for coating.

Bring the cream to the boil in a pan, then remove from the heat and gradually add the 400g dark chocolate and the black chocolate, stirring with a whisk until melted and the mixture is smooth. Stir in the butter and cider brandy. Transfer to a bowl and leave to cool, then chill for 1–1½ hours or until the mixture is firm enough to spoon into rough shapes.

Spoon the truffle mixture onto a tray lined with cling film in rough mounds. Leave in the fridge until firm.

Melt the reserved chocolate in a bowl over a pan of simmering water. Take off the heat and let cool for a few minutes. Sift the cocoa powder onto a tray; have a third clean tray ready for the finished truffles.

Using a thin skewer or cocktail stick, dip each truffle quickly into the melted chocolate, allow the excess to drain off, then put into the cocoa powder, shaking the tray so the truffle becomes coated. When half of the truffles are coated, shake off excess cocoa and lay on the clean tray.

Store the truffles in a sealed plastic container lined with kitchen paper in the fridge (no longer than a month… as if). Take them out of the fridge about half an hour before serving to bring to room temperature.

HIX OYSTER ALE CAKE

This is a nice, rich teatime cake that is also very good served with cheese. If you can't find my dark oyster ale, I'll allow you to use Guinness, stout or a porter.

Serves 8–10

60g sultanas
a little softened butter for greasing
450g self-raising flour, sifted
a good pinch of salt
a good pinch of freshly grated nutmeg
a good pinch of mixed spice
a good pinch of ground cinnamon
225g molasses sugar
225g cold butter, cut into small cubes
finely grated zest of 2 oranges
finely grated zest of 1 lemon
1 free-range large egg, beaten
200ml Hix oyster ale (see above)

Put the sultanas into a bowl, pour on enough boiling water to cover and leave to soak overnight.

The next day, preheat the oven to 160°C/gas mark 3. Line a 20 x 10cm loaf tin, about 6cm deep, with buttered greaseproof paper. Drain the sultanas.

Sift the flour, salt and spices together into a bowl and stir in the sugar, then rub in the butter with your fingertips until the mixture resembles breadcrumbs. Stir in the grated orange and lemon zests, then gently mix in the egg, sultanas and ale.

Transfer the mixture to the prepared tin, spreading it evenly. Bake in the oven for 1½–1¾ hours or until golden and firm to the touch. To test, insert a fine skewer in the centre; it should come out clean.

Leave the cake in the tin for 5 minutes or so, then turn out onto a wire rack and leave to cool.

CHEESE

We are a nation of enthusiastic cheese makers and produce great cheeses that are at least on a par if not better than those from other countries, in my opinion. I reckon we are even giving our friends across the Channel a run for their money.

As a kid I wasn't really aware of the cheeses produced in the West Country; it was always Cheddar and Stilton at home, and the occasional piece of Blue Vinney – rare in those days – when my Gran could get her hands on some. Lymeswold, the soft, insipid, mild blue was considered a fancy cheese then; thankfully that one has disappeared off the cheese makers' map.

When I first worked in London around 20 years ago, cheeseboards comprised French cheeses and English Stilton – even poor old Cheddar never got a look in. I'm never quite sure in a restaurant whether the customer is looking for the grand cheese trolley with its disparate assortment of varieties, or just one or two selected cheeses. It is tricky to keep all the cheeses on a bulging trolley in prime condition and very, very difficult to control the wastage. I much prefer to offer just one or two selected cheeses; this enables us to select fine-quality cheeses at their best and serve them in prime condition.

The West Country is, of course, home to Cheddar, our most famous cheese and there are plenty of excellent farmhouse Cheddars produced on a small scale by skilled cheese makers to choose from. Among my favourites are Dorset Drum Cheddar from Denhay Farm, and Keen's and Montgomery's – both Somerset Cheddars.

Stinking Bishop is another very good West Country cheese, produced by Charles Martell. It is a washed rind cheese – washed in Perry to create a delicious, pungent cheese with a rich, creamy, oozing interior.

There are also some distinctive West Country blue cheeses made by the Ticklemore Cheese company, including Beenleigh Blue, a lovely sheep's milk cheese, and Harbourne Blue, a great goat's cheese with a crumbly texture and a powerful flavour.

I've come across great cheese makers all over the country, even within a 30-mile radius of London. Sandy Rose, for example, produces award-winning cheeses from her farm just outside Wokingham in Berkshire, including Barkham Blue (illustrated right), which was acclaimed as 'best new cheese' in its first year at the World Cheese Awards. Made from Channel Island milk, it is a distinctive cheese with a natural mould-ripened rind, rich blue flavour and smooth, buttery texture.

In addition to artisan cheese makers, we now have cheese aficionados like Juliet Harbutt and musician Alex James working together with cheese makers to produce interesting new cheeses. Their company, Evenlode Partnership, have turned out three great cheeses, including the soft goat's cheeses Little Wallop and Fairleigh Wallop, made in Somerset by Peter Humphries of White Lake cheeses. Little Wallop is washed in Julian Temperley's cider brandy and attactively wrapped in vine leaves.

Evenlode's third – and my favourite British blue cheese – is Blue Monday (illustrated left) made by Ruaraidh Stone in Tain, Scotland. To me, it compares favourably with a well-made Gorgonzola picante and I often serve it with perfectly ripe pears, honey and walnuts, or use it in salads.

The British and World Cheese awards, which I'm often asked to judge, are a great source of inspiration and the UK and Ireland always come out pretty well. It's heartening to see so many high-quality entries and there are always excellent new cheeses to put on the restaurant menus.

ACKNOWLEDGEMENTS

I'd like to thank all those who have helped to make The Oyster & Chop House such a great success: my business partner Ratnesh Bagdai and his wife Niketa; Julian Biggs, Stuart Tattershall, Rory McCoy and the rest of the restaurant staff; all of our brilliant suppliers, including Aubrey Allen, Jack O'Shea, Ben Weatherall, Billfields Food Company, Bocaddon Farm and The Wright Brothers; also artists Tim Noble and Sue Webster, Sanchita Islam, Caragh Thuring, Michael Landy and Mat Collishaw, whose work lends such character to the restaurant.

My thanks also to Quadrille Publishing, especially Publishing Director Jane O'Shea, and the freelance team who have produced this fitting tribute to the restaurant: photographer Jason Lowe, designer Lawrence Morton and editor Janet Illsley.

Finally, a very special thank you to Clare Lattin for her inspiration and continuous support.

First published in 2010 by
Quadrille Publishing Limited
Alhambra House
27-31 Charing Cross Road
London WC2H OLS

www.quadrille.co.uk

Text © 2010 Mark Hix

Photography © 2010 Jason Lowe

Design and layout © 2010 Quadrille Publishing Limited

The rights of the author have been asserted.

Cataloguing in Publication Data: a catalogue record for this book is available from the British Library.

ISBN: 978 184400 392 1

Printed in China

Publishing director Jane O'Shea
Creative director Helen Lewis
Project editor Janet Illsley
Art direction & design Lawrence Morton
Photographer Jason Lowe
Production Marina Asenjo, Vincent Smith

Mark Hix is an award-winning food writer and restaurateur. Following 17 years overseeing London's fashionable Le Caprice, The Ivy, Scott's and J. Sheekey, Mark set up on his own and now has four acclaimed restaurants in London and the West Country. In 2009, he was Tatler's Restaurateur of the Year. Mark has a weekly column in the Independent on Saturday magazine and has written eight cookbooks. His last book, British Seasonal Food, was named The Guild of Food Writers' Cookery Book of the Year in 2009.